D0928012

POUND REVISED

Pound Revised

Paul Smith

CROOM HELM
London & Canberra

© 1983 Paul Smith
Croom Helm Ltd, Provident House, Burrell Row,
Beckenham, Kent BR3 1AT

British Library Cataloguing in Publication Data

Smith, Paul
    Pound revised.
    1. Pound, Ezra – Criticism and interpretation
    I. Title
    811'.52   PS3531.082Z

    ISBN 0-7099-2346-5

Printed and bound in Great Britain by
Biddles Ltd, Guildford and King's Lynn

CONTENTS

Inscribed to Andrew

ABBREVIATIONS AND REFERENCES

Throughout this book numbers set in brackets in the body of the text (e.g. (562)) refer to *The Cantos of Ezra Pound* (New York, 1970). This edition is also published in London, by Faber & Faber, 1975, and is the most complete and correct version available.

For convenience I have also made bracketed reference to works by the four writers who appear in my text; these are abbreviated thus:

Pound
CEP   — *Collected Early Poems*
CSP   — *Collected Shorter Poems*
SP   — *Selected Prose*
LE   — *Literary Essays*
GB   — *Gaudier-Brzeska: a Memoir*
GK   — *Guide to Kulchur*
PD   — *Pavannes and Divagations*
J/M   — *Jefferson and/or Mussolini*
ABC   — *ABC of Reading*
Letters — *The Letters of Ezra Pound, 1907-1941*
EPS   — *Ezra Pound Speaking* (Radio Speeches)

Joyce
D   — *Dubliners*
U1   — *Ulysses*
FW   — *Finnegans Wake*

H.D.
ET   — *End to Torment*
TF   — *Tribute to Freud*
T   — *Trilogy*
HE   — *Helen in Egypt*
HD   — *Hermetic Definition*

Zukofsky
A   — *A, 1-24*

These abbreviations are always followed by a page number referring to the editions of the relevant works which are listed in the Bibliography.

All other references are given in footnotes. Numbers raised from the body of my text direct the reader to the notes for each chapter at the end of the text.

PREFACE

My aims in this work have been quite simple. I wanted to examine the life and work of Ezra Pound in a way which would consolidate the connections between the great and influential body of his writing and the vagaries and convictions of the man himself. Following on from this I wanted to explore the attitudes towards Pound and his writing held by some of the writers who came under his influence. I have tried to explain what sort of implicit and necessary revisions of Pound's poetics were made by James Joyce, H.D. and Louis Zukofsky.

In dealing with Pound himself, I have taken the view that the extra-literary causes which he espoused cannot finally be viewed apart from his actual writing practice and vice versa. Accordingly, I set about trying to prove that Pound's writing and language are intrinsically total-itarian. I have also tried to explicate some of the unconscious springs (which are always overdetermined and so, admittedly, never open to complete explication) which went towards making this difficult indivi-dual, Ezra Pound.

My approach to Pound's writing has been fundamentally aggressive, but I think to understand at the same time the enormous attraction of that writing to other poets and critics. Pound can sometimes be a fine writer; furthermore, here is clearly a man deeply concerned with and involved in a time of great social and literary upheaval. I take it that it is to his credit that he perceived the necessary connections between the social and the literary, and that he devoted his unquestionably enormous energy to precisely those problems. But I have found that his work and influence must be regarded with suspicion because of the very underlying assumptions that I have tried to expose here.

As counterpoise to whatever kind of attack I have been able to mount against Pound, I have also attempted to survey other writing which has had demonstrable trouble in dealing with the Poundian spectre but which has, equally, been influenced by it. It is with such writing that my sympathies lie and I have turned there in the hope of finding antidotes, or experiments towards antidotes, for what I see as the damaging implications of Pound's work.

The problem that Pound poses for criticism can perhaps be best indicated through D.C. Heymann's prefatory remarks to his book *Ezra Pound: The Last Rower*:

Pound will no doubt always be regarded as a hugely problematic figure. His supporters have tended in the past to depict him in terms most favourable to him — to emphasize the power of his poetry — but have ignored some of the paramount concerns — economic and political — that plagued him during a major portion of his life. Conversely, there are those more interested in the fact that he was an anti-Semite, a drumbeater for Hitler and Mussolini, than they are in coming to terms with his poetry. The poetry, let us not forget, is difficult and often obscure; it is much easier to think of Pound as a political fanatic and to dismiss his verse as the work of a madman.

It is exactly the division that Heymann talks of which beleaguers much Poundian criticism, and I have attempted to harmonise the division in some way. What seems to me to have been missing from what is now a thriving scholarly industry is any but the vaguest attempt to relate the poetry to the politics — a task which I think necessarily involves some theoretical notion of what happens between a body and its language. If I have tried to import such a theory into my work it is not an entirely unprecedented step: I have been stimulated by the work of Marcelin Pleynet, Maud Ellmann and A.E. Durant, all of whose writings draw quite heavily on the work of the French psychoanalyst Jacques Lacan, and on modern critical thought generally. To some extent I too have followed this course.

Lacan, in particular, has done much to provide a theoretical background for dealing with this question of the individual's relation to language, a question which seems especially pertinent to Pound and his work since Pound was claiming to be producing a new language for poetry. Consequently, I have utilised what I understand Lacan to be talking about, but I have done so in a manner which might require some vindicatory remarks. It seems to me that Lacan suffers greatly at the hands of many literary critics wishing to *use* him; there is often an implicit assumption in their work which is fundamentally positivist — it assumes that Lacan is expounding an immutable and so recuperable theory. (Even A.E. Durant's work, which I admire, seems to spend as much time getting Lacan in some sense right as it does on Pound's work.) I do not feel that Lacan is quite the writer to use in this manner — his celebrated 'style' is, after all, designed in part to thwart recuperation of his thinking into some discourse available for consumption under the heading 'Lacanian theory.' So I have tried to attach Lacan to my text in a sort of tangential fashion, using his words to inspissate my own. The same approach has been adopted with regard to other writers, such as Jacques Derrida. In any case, I feel that the influence of such people has been sufficiently felt by literary criticism for me to be able to avoid reductive explanation of their work.

My approach has, in short, wanted to avoid rushing to writers such as the above for the *authority* of their voice. For many reasons — not least my own imaginary identifications, and the conventional demands placed upon any critical writing — I have inevitably failed in this attempt. I am well aware, then, of the fettered irony that my rhetorical and moral attack on Pound generates. Mine is, on one important level, a strategic enterprise, designed to defuse the threat that I feel from Pound's work, and to encourage the warmth that I enjoy in Joyce, H.D. and Zukofsky.

Much work that has its roots in modern critical theory has been fascinated by Joyce, and it is to him that I first turn for indications as to what anti-Poundian writing might look like. Especially in *Finnegans Wake*, Joyce seems to provide the opposite extremity to Pound's extremist writing practice; I have tried to explain why and how this is the case. Of course, Joyce was a correspondent of Pound's and was obliged to place his work in a literary 'avant-garde' which was largely governed by Pound. Pound's hostility to Joyce's later work has helped me to understand and appreciate (to read) Joyce's work in a particular manner: it is exactly this that I wanted to write down.

H.D. and Zukofsky, being a woman and a Jew respectively, are thereby immediately plunged into some sort of conflict with Pound — be it overt or not. It is partly for this reason that I have found their work enlightening and useful. Of course, I might have chosen writers from the same categories, such as Stein or Oppen, but it is in H.D. and Zukofsky that I find the heaviest marks of Pound's influence (literary and personal) and the most significant strains that the task of writing a way out of that influence has imposed. In other words, I have wanted to describe the effects on their writing practices that Pound can be seen to have had. Indeed, all three of the writers in my counterbalance seem to have had to undertake that task of re-writing Pound, writing a way out of his shadow. It is their ways of doing this, and their relative degrees of success, that have interested me here. All three, I think, point in different directions in terms of future writing practices, but they each provide some major indication of what writing in this century could and should do with Pound and his work.

ACKNOWLEDGMENTS

The writing of this work has indebted me to many people. Michael Grant, especially, has been the source of valuable advice and encouragement as well as of warmth and generosity. Stephen Bann and David Ellis have also given much-needed advice and friendship. Other people to whom I record my gratitude are Alan Durant, Bernard Sharratt and Graham Clarke.

The book was prepared for publication while I held a Killam Postdoctoral Fellowship at Dalhousie University. I would like especially to acknowledge four members of the English department there who have defended me and my work: Alan Kennedy, Mike Klug, Andy Wainwright and Ron Huebert.

Finally, my love and thanks to Andrew and Catherine for helping me through it all, and for much else; and, of course, to my parents.

Acknowledgments

short extracts, as detailed in the footnotes; and excerpts from Ezra Pound's Broadcasts — Copyright © 1942 by the Trustees of the Ezra Pound Literary Property Trust.

Permission has also been given by the Trustees of the Ezra Pound Literary Property Trust through Faber & Faber Ltd, London, and New Directions Publishing Corporation, New York: to reprint 'Old Zuk' from 'Three Poems', *The European*, vol. 12, Copyright © 1959 by the Trustees of the Ezra Pound Literary Property Trust and to reproduce decorative initials by Henry Strater for Cantos 4 and 10 from *A Draft of XVI Cantos of Ezra Pound* in the Three Mountains Press edition, 1925, Copyright 1925 by the Trustees of the Ezra Pound Literary Property Trust, and to print the previously unpublished letter by Ezra Pound to William Bird, Copyright © 1982 by the Trustees of the Ezra Pound Literary Property Trust.

PART ONE

'No more desire flayeth me:'
Ezra Pound, 'Threnos'

1 INTRODUCTION: EARLY POUND

(i) Materiality

Near the start of his poetic career, in 1911, Ezra Pound pointed out with obvious distaste that over two hundred years of poetry in English 'had been merely the vehicle . . . the ox-cart and post-chaise for transmitting thoughts poetic or otherwise' (LE 11). This remark constitutes a call for the development of a new kind of poetic consciousness in which a consistent awareness of the primacy of poetic language − its nature, possibilities and limitations − might overrule an older kind of poetics, one which had respectfully conceived of poetry as a passive means towards the representation of humanistic thought and perception. I intend to argue here that Pound began his career with this impassioned concern for poetry 'as an art of verbal music' (LE 292), and that, even though his later work assumes an increasingly onerous load to be conveyed in the reader's direction, he at least initially was interested in this special primacy and autonomy of poetic language above all else. Such an interest encourages Pound's whole attempt to realign poetic practice, and arises specifically, it seems to me, from a firm intuition into the writing of his immediate poetic forebears, namely poets such as Browning, Morris, the Pre-Raphaelites and the Decadents, but especially Swinburne.

Much of what Pound assimilated from those poets is displayed in his *Collected Early Poems*. From the early books that are collected in that volume (such as *A Lume Spento, Exultations* and *Canzoni*) Pound made a definitive selection for his *Personae* of 1916, the volume which can now be said to define the canon and which is printed in *Collected Shorter Poems*. Some of the work repressed from the later collections Pound described as 'stale creampuffs'[1] when they were reprinted in the 1960s. Most critics seem to have agreed with Pound's estimate of these rejected pieces and have confined their investigation of them to, broadly speaking, comparing them with the work of their ancestors and to remarking what traces remain of one or two stylistic or thematic elements derived from previous poetry.

This critical procedure, a scanning of the superficial residues, has led to what I understand as a peripheral concern being elevated to a main attention, while a perhaps more important consideration has been put aside. What I think principally emanates from late-nineteenth-century verse, and what Pound's early work reduplicates, is precisely a concern for the artifice of poetic production and an ensuing respect for the autonomy of the language of poetry: both of these elements enter Pound's writing in a much more solid and formative manner than do any of the superficial elements that the critics point to. Whereas these early stylistic and thematic influences have most often been extirpated (or considerably refined) by the time of the *Cantos*, what does remain as an upshot for Pound's entire creative output is the question of the condition and status of autonomous poetic language.

There is a clear *reflexive* quality to many of Pound's early poems; it is a quality which works somewhat against the processes of poetic *reflection* which are familiar from the work of, say, the Decadents. Pound's attention to the peculiarities and differing registers of the poetic voice as it undertakes the creation of specific music and form is perhaps most simply illustrated in the continual references he makes to the poet's own activity. This is most usually done by stress on the verbs of saying, singing or writing, or by intertextual allusion to previous writing — to Browning in 'Mesmerism' (CEP 17) for example — or by a mixture of both. To put it another way, there is a recurrent positioning of the poet in relation to his materials; sometimes this is almost over-determinedly explicit, as in the instruction that 'Canzon' is 'To be sung beneath a window' (CEP 136). This insistence on the very process and situation of utterance derives in part from Pound's fondness for the troubadour tradition with its conventions of self-conscious reference to both poet and song, the value of the latter residing in the degree of efficiency with which it is constructed (since, there, it is a commodity, an object of exchange, offered in return for food and shelter). Pound often carries these conventions, and the malcontent narrative that accompanies them, into his early work.

An example of what I am describing is to be seen in 'Cino' (CEP 10), a poem overtly concerned with the terms of its own production; first, it is *located* on 'the open road', and so explicitly outside of all the places where the song would actually be performed, but precisely there where it has gestation and birth — the scene of its production. The intention expressed in the first few lines to 'sing of the sun' is approached in the final few stanzas. Yet these stanzas, once performed, are displaced by a further and different expression of intent:

> I will sing of the white birds
> In the blue waters of heaven,
> The clouds that are spray to its sea.

Those lines forecast yet another song while still remaining part of a song themselves — first, as part of Cino's supposed utterance, and also as part of Pound's own utterance, the poem 'Cino'.

There is an unusual layering of discourse going on here, and its workings are further revealed in the respective textual arrangements of this poem in its earlier printed versions (in *A Lume Spento*, for example) and in *Collected Shorter Poems*. The latter version, by altering the line indentations and the inverted commas which locate the different discourse in the early versions, deliberately includes the above three lines within Cino's own song. The earlier text, on the other hand, quite clearly excludes them. This I take to underline Pound's strategem of demonstrating the process whereby two different utterances or more can be included in and mixed with a third in order to emphasise and play with their relativity as differing registers of language. Here, such play is further highlighted by the appearance of other identifiable discourses, the reporting and mimicking of the words of the courtly women.

It is precisely this sort of *play* that seems to me to be of paramount interest in this poem, since it is a direct consequence of the simple fact that language is allowed to be aware of itself and of its many layers and registers within the poem's genesis — aware, indeed, of its whole role in the production of meanings. This aspect makes the poem less obviously just 'an exercise in Browningesque monologue':[2] Browning is never so daring. Pound seems here deliberately to attempt the display of possibilities in the different levels of utterance that go to make a single artificial structure. The artificial nature of the construct is not disavowed.

If Pound imported some notion of the reflexive potentiality in language production from his work on the troubadours he was not slow in recognising kindred qualities in Swinburne's writing. It is, apparently, the critical consensus that Pound 'sounds worst when most Swinburnian'[3] — even though few of his poems can be said to follow the lines of a Swinburnian stylistics. And although it might ultimately be correct to think that Pound's interest in Swinburne was not entirely technical but in a poet who seemed to ask 'the final questions about the fate of Man',[4] Swinburne's thematic influence is not especially discernible in his early work. In short, then, the critics do not offer much evidence of Pound's thematic debt to Swinburne, even though the latter figures in Pound's writing by way of allusion much more than any other poet. And surely Pound's proposition in the essay 'Swinburne versus his Biographers' should not be ignored: that 'No one else has made such music in English . . . ' (LE 293).

Perhaps the question of Swinburne's status for Pound can be resolved in Pound's strong dislike for the 'muzziness . . . softness' (LE 363) that characterises the nineties and the verse of the Decadents after their fall from Swinburnian heights. The Decadents demonstrably reversed the step forward that Swinburne offered in his realisation of the priority of poetic language and in his ostentatious refusal to allow writing to be subservient to the expression of poetic reflection and impression. What the young Pound learned from him, then, can be said to lie precisely in this trenchant attitude to the very materiality of writing, its activity. The Decadents are especially reprehensible to Pound because of their persistence in a writing aesthetic that Swinburne's effort could have relegated to desuetude. A comparison of a typical Decadent poem to one by Swinburne should illustrate what I am proposing.

I take it that the doyen of the Decadent movement, Arthur Symons, is not misrepresented by his poem-sequence of 1892, 'At Dieppe'.[5] This is a sequence of six poems whose movement may be traced by the first, second and final pieces, which I quote:

1. *After Sunset*
   The sea lies quieted beneath
   The after-sunset flush
   That leaves upon the heaped grey clouds
   The grape's faint purple blush.

   Pale, from a little space in heaven
   Of delicate ivory,
   The sickle moon and one gold star
   Look down upon the sea.

2. *On the Beach*
   Night, a grey sky, a ghostly sea,
   The soft beginning of the rain:
   Black on the horizon, sails that wane
   Into·the distance mistily.

   The tide is rising; I can hear
   The soft roar broadening far along,
   As, deep through depths of sleep, a song
   Borne inward to a dreamy ear.

Softly the stealthy night descends;
The black sails fade into the sky.
Is this not, where the sea-line ends,
The shore-line of infinity?

I cannot think or dream: the grey
Unending waste of sea and night,
Dull, impotently infinite,
Blots out the very hope of day.

6. *Requies*

O is it death or life
That sounds like something strangely known
In this subsiding out of strife,
This slow sea-monotone?

A sound, scarce heard through sleep,
Murmurous as the August bees
That fill the forest hollows deep
About the roots of trees.

O is it life or death,
O is it hope or memory,
That quiets all things with this breath
Of the eternal sea?

The particularity of the title that Symons gives the sequence sets the whole very much within a real, definable world, and so it is not surprising to find that the first of these poems is just two simple quatrains describing the sea and sky at evening in a speedy, impressionistic piling-up of small details — establishing what, finally, is a somewhat anodyne vignette. The representational mechanisms here are quite familiar and little remarkable.

While the first poem is purely descriptive, representational, the second broadens the perspective in order to intensify the mood: 'The tide is rising', and so on. But in place of the descriptive verbs of the first poem the second admits the authorial 'I' as it asserts its central position, its status as virtual pole within the scene. This emergence of the 'I' acts as a further broadening of perspective and may be said to describe the poet's intellectual powers at work on what is reflected into the eye. It is, of course, the essence of Decadent poetry that this eye should have a languid view of the world, one which (as my description of these pieces as vignettes might indicate) should be almost indistinct, peripheral, floating off at the edges of the picture, precipitated by the careless 'I cannot think or dream'.

The three poems which lead up to the final 'Requies' continue to evoke the same mood and provide an explanation for its lethargy – a woman: 'I lie and watch the sea and think of her.' The final poem underlines and intensifies the whole sequence, filling it out by providing a sententious and general support. 'Requies' is, quite literally, reflective: the poet offers his reflections on an unproblematically graspable vista, and distorts that scene into a hackneyed question as to its meaning for human eyes and minds. While the first two poems try to send the reader to construct a world that exists – Dieppe – the last does no more than impose a particular kind of human reflection on the information that is reflected on to the eye.

These poems, miming a particular Victorian mode of seeing and comprehending the world, work as examples of what Symons himself calls 'Impressionistic writing'. He claims that it is 'an interesting heresy of a particular kind of art to seek truth before beauty': a heresy not, of course, to be found in his own work where scenes are set firmly, properly motivated,before significance (Symons' 'truth') is allowed to enter and complete the plenitude of the poetic offering. Symons also describes that impressionism as being concerned with 'revelation, the re-creation, of a coloured and harmonious world which . . . owes its very existence to the eyes that see it':[6] we can tell very well what kind of misty eyes are being set to this task.

What always remains conspicuously absent from Symons' writing about writing is any account of the *poesis*, the very doing of the poem. This is because, in effecting their brand of late Victorian recreation, starting with beauty and transmuting it to truth by means of the alchemical quatrain, Symons and his colleagues make the flat and unquestioned assumption that the organisation of poetic language into artificial forms involves nothing more problematic than the easy utilisation of a system of convenience and restraint, a system which can furnish the proper receptacle for the observations and ruminations that pour from the poetic sensibility.

Such an aesthetic relegates writing, as Pound began by complaining, to a mere vehicularism. Nothing could be further from such a use of the particular qualities of poetic writing than the work of Swinburne. His 'Rondel' may be taken to illustrate the difference:

Kissing her hair I sat against her feet,
Wove and unwove it, wound and found it sweet;
Made fast therewith her hands, drew down her eyes,
4 Deep as deep flowers and dreamy like dim skies;
With her own tresses bound and found her fair,
    Kissing her hair.

7 Sleep were no sweeter than her face to me,
Sleep of cold sea-bloom under the cold sea;
9 What pain could get between my face and hers?
10 What new sweet thing would love not relish worse?
11 Unless, perhaps, white death had kissed me there,
    Kissing her hair?[7]

This poem is set in a form which is by definition self-enclosing, which has a necessary circularity. The question mark at the end of the poem seems to emphasise that some modulation in the three words that have to be repeated must occur: my reading of 'Rondel' involves chasing that modulation from the first and through the second stanza to demonstrate that the easy articulation of poetic observation and reflection is not available to Swinburne and produces in the attempt precisely this question mark for poetic writing.

The first stanza, on the face of it, is well formed, a grammatical poetic utterance in that it follows its set form, is rhythmically regular, is euphonious and self-enclosing: there is a recognisable and solid iambic metre, varied by dactyls and anapaests, and there is a strict homogeneity of sound, epitomised by the close phonological relationships between the end-rhyme words. One might even be tempted to suggest that the very sense of the stanza lies in its correct articulation of this formal frame. Yet there are signs of a definite breakdown in that sense, and the breakdown will occur in the second stanza. The reference to the weaving and unweaving of the woman's hair is a quiet reminder of the classical metaphor for writing, now enjoined by our fashonable word 'text'. This submerged metaphor accompanies the self-consciousness that inevitably attends such a strict form as the rondel, with the result that Swinburne might appear to be concerned as much with the poem's actual matter of production as with the woman's hair.

The first stanza's central image of erotic bondage with the woman's hair (the hair − the language perhaps − already given as a fetishised object, to be kissed) induces a sort of vertigo at the enormity of its own realisation and has the effect of beginning to unbalance the writing's certainty. Here the author's dreamy derangement (signalled by the description of the woman's eyes in line 4) gives way to a realisation of the act of bondage in the grammatically unstable line, 'With her own tresses bound and found her fair'. That momentary imbalance is the signal — to be amplified in the next stanza — of language's unease at being caught up in such a formal container, caught in its own tresses as it were.

Although the second stanza might appear to be the counterpart of Symons' 'Requies' — a rumination on a scene that has been set — it does in fact mark the fall of the language into a strange uncertainty that is quite different from Symons' confident reflection. The first sign of this is in the retreat of the verbs into the subjunctive and conditional, away from the indicative act of the first stanza. There follows a break-down of the technical standards previously set: the rhythms fall into ambiguity, or revert to a bland iambic form (as in lines 9 and 10). Where the sounds of the first stanza had been phonologically and semantically worked for, the sudden intrusion into this stanza of words like 'sleep' and 'pain' is not. The poem's previous certainty is under-mined, not least by the questioning tone that the last few lines adopt. The questions, in lines 9 and 10, are perhaps indicative of the text's unease as it asks 'What next?' What can 'get between my face and hers' to generate an ending to the poem as it attempts to incorporate the words 'kissing her hair' which now have become questionable after the realisation of their image's fetishistic power? It is in these questions that the self-consciousness of the form and language that Swinburne uses reaches a peak. And the result is the fall into the quasi-nonsense of 'What new sweet thing would love not relish worse' and the grammatical non-sequitur of the final 'Unless . . . ' clause (line 11). But it is perhaps in that confused juxtaposition of positives and nega-tives in line 10 that the whole uncertainty of language's status is most clearly enacted.

So, the strict form of this poem seems actually to foreground the fact of writing itself and invites the reader to look closely at the way language plays, escaping in some sense its subject matter and its author. At any rate, once the specific signs of the writing process are brought to the poem's surface as symptoms in the way I have described, the text can palpably no longer function in the way that most Victorian verse imagines: the reflective possibilities of writing are replaced by the reflexive. It is important for what I have to say later to notice that this is not simply a question of technique or changes in technique: it is an epistemological question about the behaviour of language and demands a fully different order of attention from both reader and writer.

Pound's lesson from Swinburne, then, far from being an overt thematic one, resides in this recognition of the materiality of language and its tendency to break the barriers of that view of poetry which wishes to see language as simply a vehicle. This is clearly not a lesson that Pound was likely to learn from most of the poets of the nineties, and yet it pervades his own work most strongly in its early stages. The reflexive strain in his early writings lays great emphasis on the particular qualities of poetic language and poetic technique – on the materiality of language and general poetic procedures. Pound's own 'Roundel for Arms', for instance, is specifically addressed to 'my words' (CEP 234). Pound makes no bones about informing us that we are dealing with an artefact, a song, a stylised utterance which has an autonomy and contingency of its own, not always recuperable to a world of meanings that are fixed in reflection.

Many of Pound's other early poems include this explicit self-observation, some even in such a manner as to suggest that the song itself is a channel of perception, rather than a container for the reflection of light from the visible world. For example, another 'Roundel' addresses a woman

> Who art the soul of beauty and whose praise
> Or colour or light or song championeth. (CEP 234)

There is more than a slight suggestion here that the song itself may act upon the wordly object in the same way as colour or light (which is signally active here, rather than reflective). It is the nature of the fore-grounding of poetic materiality to emphasise what language can *do* (and we clearly have not to forget the root of the word 'poetry' in *poien*).

Such a foregrounding might be best epitomised by Pound's 'Canzon' (CEP 136/7). The theme of this piece is particularly banal and, after the statement of it in the first stanza, the poem relies on and fore-grounds references to 'these my phrases', to the 'tuneful words . . . words unworthy' uttered by 'my voice'. Such references move the reader's attention from the plain theme and direct us to the poem's very careful and elaborate formal devices. Indeed,the realignment of our attention is effected in the very first line where the sense might well have been generated on purely phonological grounds:

> Heart mine, art mine, whose embraces
> Clasp but wind that past thee bloweth? (CEP 136)

There is in the word 'art' an initially seductive ambiguity which attaches itself to the reflexive strain I have been pointing to. The reading process is here drawn to where Pound's own attention appears to have been. Here it is towards the repeated 'a' and 'o' sounds, to the unusual triple-rhyme scheme, initiated in 'embraces . . . traces . . . amazes', whose sounds are repeated in each stanza, and to the carefully modulated rhythms which these formal features encourage. In other words, these stanzas, proposing or foregrounding their own processes, result in an almost 'triumphant evasion of substance'.[8]

It is noteworthy that 'Canzon' — along with most of the other work in the 1911 *Canzoni* — was suppressed from later collections as Pound became less and less willing to indulge what he clearly thought of as nothing more than an apprentice's taste for literary experiment. There are, of course, many poems in the later *Personae* collection which still exhibit signs of the concerns I have dealt with: 'Cino' is still there, along with 'Villonaud' and 'Famam Librosque Cano' which speculates as to the fate of the finished product of the poet's labours. But although there still remain these texts which 'behold how black immortal ink/ Drips from my deathless pen' (CEP 181), most such early investigations have been removed, underlining that, despite beginning with this con-cern for materiality, Pound (for reasons I shall now deal with) finished by wishing systematically to repress that whole vein in his work.

(ii) Substance

Pound's incipient reluctance to use those of his poems which fore-ground the fact of poetic utterance can be measured in even such an early poem as 'Praise of Ysolt' (1909). Although that poem insists on itself as its own subject matter (its refrain, 'song, a song' fixes the whole utterance inside the consciousness of a song's nativity), a certain resentment against the nagging refrain emerges:

> But his answer cometh, as winds and as lutany,
> As a vague crying upon the night
> That leaveth me no rest, saying ever,
> > 'Song, a song' (CEP 79)

The reluctance here prefigures Pound's later attempts to suppress the whole vein of materiality that I have described. So, indeed, does his quite amusing attempt in his essay on Swinburne to pass over the older poet's lessons in order to praise him for his supposed universal concerns: Swinburne's refusal of any 'facile solution for his universe' (LE 294) leads Pound to praise him in 'Salve O Pontifex' where he appears as the priestly poet unravelling the secret of life as he looks 'out into the infinitude/Of the blue waves of heaven' (CEP 40). The attempt to see such concerns as Swinburne's principal ones ignores his ability to turn the reader's attention to forms and language (a language which is 'very much alive with this singular life of its own').[9]

Pound's 1915 preface to the poems of Lionel Johnson may also be taken as part of this repressive syndrome. There, the 'traditionalist of traditionalists' (LE 361) is praised for his craftsmanship, and we see how the consciousness of the inescapable self-presentation of the poetic act begins to be devalued, diluted in Pound's mind to be replaced by this much less charged notion — that of craft. It is an idea that is amplified by Pound's statement that he had 'resolved that at thirty I would know more about poetry than any man living, that I would know the dynamic content from the shell, that I would know what was accounted poetry everywhere'.[10] Such a disdain for the 'shell' and the preference for the dynamism of content legislate quite clearly against the recognition of the primacy of poetic materiality. In similar vein, Pound, the professional poet, praises Johnson for his 'hatred of amateurism' (LE 363). In other words, Pound was interested at this point in redeveloping a notion of the master craftsman (with both words of the phrase carrying their weight) in order to defuse the power of poetic materiality.

It is with the distinctions that this new category allows him that Pound begins to redefine poetry so that materiality will finally not distort substance — in other words, to build a stronger vehicle for whatever substance the poet might wish to communicate. In the establishment of this project the preface to Johnson was an exceptionally important turning point; on this new path Pound has to cross a paradox. His writing had attempted to encourage materiality, and now, in refusing to take the risks that formalism offers in its attempts to evade substance, it tries to establish within the poem what we might call a social space — by which I mean that his poems emerge from formalistic imaginations, epitomised by many of the poems from *Canzoni*, and they thence move towards the relative urbanity and social comment that can be found, for example, in 'Hugh Selwyn Mauberley'.

The early poems had obviously served as an arena for experimentation (for finding new things, in accordance with the troubadour tradition) and as the locus for, in Andrew Crozier's phrase, 'systematically developing a mastery of the syllable'. But the fate of most of this early work was excision from the canon, on the grounds that such writing can say 'nothing in particular'.[11] The play of language, the privileging of the signifier over the signified, no longer appears sufficient to Pound, and so in his Imagist and Vorticist periods he embarks upon a programme designed to efface the power of the signifier and replace it with a controlled and mastered language – one which supposedly can come into unambiguous contact with the truth of the world. Privilege is now given to substance over language and so Pound is obliged to search out some means of controlling the writing energy that he had previously cultivated in order to force language to fulfil the substantial demands that he will increasingly place upon it.

Crozier's use of the phrase 'mastery of the syllable' is especially appropriate in its wording: Pound's concern for the materiality and the 'minutiae of his craft' (LE 6) no longer wishes to countenance language's freedom and play, rather it wishes to obtain a mastery over it in the interests of a poem's content. His much-vaunted 'craft [taking] the shape of the line as its base'[12] and his 'reconstituting the verse-line as the poetic unit . . . in such a way that smaller components within the line (down to the very syllable) can recover weight and value'[13] is no longer a celebration of the autonomy of poetic language, but more nearly its oppression: the throwing of the reader's attention back to separate syllables is designed now to throw him back to Pound's specific meaning, back to reflection. As Pound himself admits when talking of his intentions in the *Cantos*,

> I hope that the reader has not understood it straight off. I should like to invent some kind of typographical dodge which would force the reader to stop and *reflect* for five minutes (or five hours), to go back to the facts mentioned and think over their *significance* for himself (my emphases).[14]

This tendency towards stressing the poem's social space is not simply a mechanical one but corresponds to a drafting of Pound's special view of the social world. The move away from the interiorisation of meaning and the concomitant awareness of the reflexivity of poetic discourse seem to occur between the publication of *Canzoni* in 1911 and the appearance of the first cantos in 1917. The most important work that Pound published in the interim is *Lustra*, in which the tensions between materiality and substance are fully at work. Although no longer treating us to poems the like of 'Canzon', this book none the less contains some work which manages to suggest the surfacing of the poetic process, but Pound's overriding concern is with substance, with the content that the external world might provide.

The sort of poems I am referring to are able to move in and out of poetic fact. This is simply a measure of their mixed concern, and is evident in poems such as 'Salutation the Second', which talks about the destiny of what the poet writes (CSP 94), or like 'Commission' (CSP 97), which can only carry itself out after the by now familiar reference to the mobility of 'my songs'. These two poems constitute part of the system of punctuation in *Lustra* which serves to point up the other poems in the collection with a different drive — that of replacing the banal and almost negligible subject matter of the early poems with definite and solid 'verisimilitudes' (CSP 91). Thus Pound presumably intends to deal with the social and aesthetic issues of his time in a direct confrontation, one configured here by the juxtaposition of these two types of poem. Merely the titles of some of the later, revisionist poems can help locate the parameter of Pound's concerns: 'The Coming of War', 'Society', 'Shop Girl', 'L'Art 1910', 'The Social Order' and so on.

It is in such socially oriented poems that the new Poundian poetics of 'direct treatment' (LE 3) properly emerges. It is a poetics which rests upon the assumption that poetry can in some sense get to the heart of the matter, of things — objects, emotions, experiences, opinions, et cetera — indeed, upon the assumption that these things can actually have existence outside of the utterance that posits them. Thus, it is a poetics which does not recognise the rich armatures of the whole problematic of language's relation to the phenomenal world; more specifically, it works against the notion that the world arrives with us through the mediation of language and can even be said to be created for consciousness by language. This is an elision of Pound's previous recognition of language's autonomy and only now assumes its pre-eminence in his writing procedures. Previously, the concern for formulated artifice and for language's specificity suggested other kinds of work.

And now the Imagist theory which Pound helped to construct can be seen to refuse the implications of Pound's earlier writings. It will not subscribe to the view that we have our notion of things through the agency of language. That whole area of refusal leads to Pound's celebrated phrase which tells us that 'the image itself is the speech' (GB 88). Such an idea, relying on a belief that language in some way covers its object, brings Pound theoretically full circle to the position that his early poems had implicitly been subverting, namely to the representational ethic where language is seen as simply the vehicle for the reflection of something extra-textual.

In some ways the flaws of the Imagists' perspective are given the lie by actual Imagist practice, or even by the story that Pound himself tells of the genesis of the very poem so often taken to be the epitome of Imagism, 'In a Station of the Metro':

> The apparition of these faces in the crowd;
> Petals on a wet, black bough. (CSP 119)

The fact that Pound can give such an account of this poem as we find in his essay 'How I Began' (and later in *Gaudier-Brzeska*), which includes a version of the poem's experiential impulse and explanation of the process leading to the writing of the poem after 'well over a year',[15] should tell us to be suspicious of a theory which claims that language, properly handled, gets straight to its object. Rather it seems that Pound's searching for 'words for what this made me feel', and the reporting of preliminary, longer versions of the poem, is simply the story of a search for a technique: indeed, this searching for words to express feelings is, epistemologically, bound up with the whole tradition of Western art. Indeed, on one level this poem is no more than the result of a reworking of those traditional modes by a series of magisterial reductions (from prose version, through longer poems, to 'image'). The Imagist expediency of saying that words can focus on reality if handled well is also overtly traditional, and surely no more than a way of saying that we need to know the correct, efficient techniques in language in order to write: for Pound the correct method would consist in reductions and condensations, metonymic fragmentations and metaphoric leaps, all of which will become more familiar procedures in the *Cantos*.

The limitations of the epistemological changes made by Imagism are exposed in the theoretical insistence that, in May Sinclair's words, 'Presentation, not representation, is the watchword of the school.'[16] Sinclair's phrase unwittingly acknowledges that the world is seen and observed by words in its use of 'watchword'. Imagism is (epistemologically) *representational* in a sense that she herself underlines when she claims that the empirical observations available to someone who has stood 'on a hill, in or under a pine-wood when it is tossed about by the wind' can vindicate H.D.'s poem 'Oread' which deals with this situation. Yet in the sentence quoted above, she deliberately and tendentiously repressed the 're-' of 'representation' simply to give the Imagists the apparently revolutionary adjective 'presentative' and thus to vaunt their simple changes in poetic techniques.

Indeed, in some lights the whole Imagist project can be seen as simply a similar sort of truncatory exercise. William Empson, for example, sees it that way in regard to simple, traditional representation: he emphasises that Imagist technique consists in nothing other than the lopping off of the logical stays of connected discourse, and thus presents the reader with a linguistic utterance that is unusual only in that it needs to have its experiential base deduced, rather than explained in the old manner.[17] Such a view finds support in Pound's own reductive view of what he thinks happens to an experiential object in the course of its inscription: 'Emotion, *seizing* upon some external scene or action, carries it in fact to the mind; that vortex *purges* it of all save the essential *dominant* or dramatic qualities and *it emerges like the external original*' (SP 345; my emphases). For Pound, the process of writing increasingly consists in these purgatorial, dominating and finally representational processes.

Pound's Imagism, then, relies on a belief that a certain technique in language will allow language to embody the world and become efficiently denotative, capable of reproducing an external origin quite simply. As David Simpson puts it, this involves a 'realist' poetry which 'stands in an authoritarian relationship to its readers. It demands reception, it does not invite or necessitate interpretation.'[18] What it offers, in effect, is tautological, an image of 'the external original' purged of all its phenomenological encumbrances. In other words, Imagism was a poetic ideology based upon a technique of reduction ('In a Station of the Metro' is a fine example of how reductive metonymy works) and whose only novelty was in its rejection of some of the standard prerequisites of poetic utterance, namely logical progression of thought, supply of connectives, pre-ordained form, rhythm, metre and so on. In its epistemology Imagist poetry does not in fact differ from its most hated forebears in so far as it implies that poetry should accurately reflect, without surplus, the material world: all of which leaves us with a conclusion that John Gould Fletcher was acute enough to arrive at at the time: 'Imagisme is an attitude towards technique pure and simple'[19] and so the school's propaganda and manifestos may be seen as simply the justifications for changes in technique which cover a return to representation and its ichnographic ethic.

(i) Communication

As Pound's writing increasingly takes upon itself the task of filling its material container with a substance, it strangely adopts the image of the vortex to describe itself (see Figure I). The vortex, an empty centre with the energies of poetic writing whirling around it, might seem to be more appropriate for the description of Pound's earlier work since the drive of the later work is increasingly towards the very filling of that empty centre. Indeed, it is no surprise to find the vortex image subsequently reappear in altered form in Pound's later work: it is transformed to the famous 'rose in the steel dust image' (449).

In that revised image lines of force are traced around, and blossom from a fixed and solid centre. This centre is the dominating power of the magnet as it guides and controls the steel filings which are subjected in a relationship of force. This change from vortex to magnet images confirms the re-assumption of control as the aim of Pound's work — an aim which is totally at odds with the implicit epistemology and poetics of his early experiments. The later image acts as the mark for Pound's filling his work with societal content, and thus with a sense that has its origin in an experiential pressure and presence which exerts an oppressive power over language's proper autonomy. Pound's poetics now strives towards what would be merely an illusion — and a traditional illusion, at that — of the sufficiency and plenitude of poetic discourse.

We might say that a traditional view of art would start out with the solidity that the magnet in this image represents — with, in other words, a certain *doxa* — and would control the patterning of energies as they emerge from that central control. For Pound a temporal priority or the very particular historical circumstances he lived brought about a discovery of some qualities of writing energy before his sights were set in any but an obscure and insecure manner on the magnet. I take it that the fierce, feverish supervision that Pound's major poetry thence exerts on the magnet is such as to compensate for his early nonchalant attitude towards it.

Statements that Pound himself makes can help to underscore the importance to him of this centralising drive. It is, for example, apparent in his comparison between his homeland and the capital cities of

Figure I

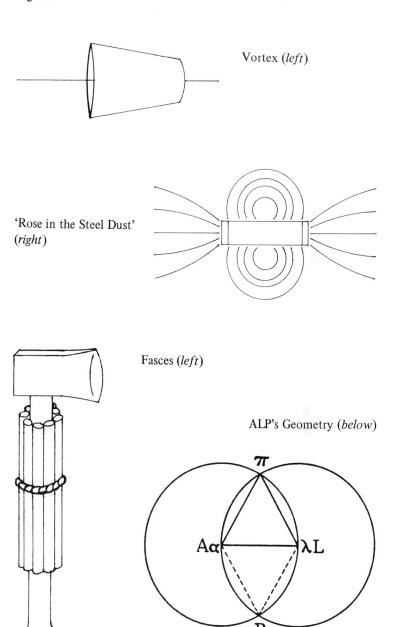

Vortex (*left*)

'Rose in the Steel Dust'
(*right*)

Fasces (*left*)

ALP's Geometry (*below*)

Europe. Paris, especially, is seen as 'this great oasis . . . this bivouac' from which intellectual worth emanates, while opposed to that he sees the 'curious teething promise of my own vast occidental nation', America. Elsewhere Pound criticises the 'decentralized state of America' for its inability to reproduce the 'sort of filtration of ideas [which] is precisely what does happen in capitals'.[1] We can see, then, that the need to reduce, to filter down and centralise is an important tendency for Pound. Indeed, the *Cantos* themselves might be seen as the hopeful embodiment of Pound's desire that an 'efficient synthesis' of all the knowledge produced by a civilisation should be effected, resulting in a 'super-thesis' every hundred years or so.[2]

This facet of Pound's thinking remains with him throughout his life and can be seen at work (along with the nostalgia, linked, which also permeates his output) when he replies to Charles Olson's questioning at St Elizabeths. Olson refers to Pound's influence in his own generation's way of 'working our way through, discarding . . . to an island such as you started from. Pound: Yes, Paris, this island. I call it the ISLE OF PARIS.'[3] In this light it is easy to see Pound's whole apprenticeship in the arts, his deliberately eclectic learning, as a preparation or a gathering of power for the project which will demonstrate the reductibility of the cultural world to some centrality or to some distilled product; thus, his work would attempt to vouch for his slogan that all the wisdom a man might need can be picked up in a day's reading. For Pound, poetry consists entirely in reduction, so that 'Dichten = Condensare' (GK 369), or in the words he borrows from T.E. Hulme, 'All a man ever thought would go into half a sheet of notepaper' (SP 238).

Such an attitude to intellectual process might best be described (playing with the 'rose in the steel dust' image once more) as centripetal. Christine Brooke-Rose has attempted to compare Pound's poetic practice with that of Langland, pointing out with some enthusiasm this very centripetal tendency in Pound's work. To do so, she deploys a model of the structural principle in *Piers Plowman*, namely the spiral. The spiral, active energy which forms a pattern around a core is clearly akin to Pound's vortex. But for Langland the centre is the perpetual focus of the energy and is constituted by a certain lived morality, which Brook-Rose dubs *'activa vita'*.[4] This she perceives in the *Cantos* too: in *Piers Plowman* the spiral movement takes the poem through alternating fields of good and evil, somewhat as Pound's poem attempts to pass through various aspects of the real towards a paradisal state. Yet there is a great difference between Pound and Langland: Pound's method arises from the policy of 'direct treatment' and, when faced with the breakdown and decadence in society in the 1920s, produces a poetry which is more aggressive than Langland's. Pound's is 'a curious blend of the direct and the allusive'.[5] The allusiveness is perhaps an act of propriety on Pound's part: the ease with which his targets can be hit does not call for the rigour and efficiency that his armoury is supposed to be capable of. The discrepancy between his fine cutting edges and the already moribund targets is great; the mores and particulars of twentieth-century society certainly do not present the same vital obstacles as Langland tried to deal with.

The extent to which the kind and degree of poetic language which Pound has evolved is unsuited to direct operations upon the social world becomes apparent in 'Hugh Selwyn Mauberley'. Since it is precisely that world which was continually calling Pound, a Siren to his writing at this juncture, that poem might well be taken as a crucial moment in the history of Pound's repressive movement, and of his attempts to give the required solid centre to his texts. If 'Mauberley' is almost a training ground for the resolution of Pound's difficulties, it is not surprising that the Malatesta cantos or the first Nuevo Mundo cantos seem more successful than 'Mauberley'. This is perhaps because there, in the biographies of Sigismundo Malatesta and Thomas Jefferson, the more suitable ingredients of the *activa vita*, energetic and morally well formed, are to be found: it is to this that Pound's language responds. A comparison of an early poem, a section from 'Mauberley' and a short passage from these earlier cantos will indicate the movement that Pound follows. And I might perhaps stress here, by way of preterition, that what very often constitutes the *activa vita* in the *Cantos* is literature itself — written items, documents (things designed to teach, precisely), letters, other books and poems and so on; in 'Mauberley' the focus is, on the other hand, something comparatively sluggish — the social mythologies and connotations that surround literary activity.

Pound's 'The Tea Shop' comes towards the end of *Lustra*, a book which carefully and deliberately places itself in the public domain, as I have noted before: Pound's title for the book, and his note to the title explaining it as 'an offering for the sins of the whole people' (CSP 90), leave us in doubt as to the area of concern. The poems here are intended as purificatory, purgatory rites to a worthless civilisation; the number, over seventy, that Pound deems necessary is perhaps an indication of the extent of both his sacerdotal enthusiasm and his disdain for the moribundity he sees before him. We might expect the self-avowed tendentiousness of such work to fall soon into the ways of a ritual rhetoric: indeed, the lamentatory tone of many of these poems can appear as a mannerism which leads directly to the unrestrained rhetoric of, for example, sections IV and V of 'Mauberley'. And the poem 'The Tea Shop' is typical, too, of the results of Pound's focusing upon the deadness of his civilisation, presenting as it does the notion of decay creeping as much into the everyday world as it does into youthfulness:

> *The Tea Shop*
> The girl in the tea shop
>   Is not so beautiful as she was,
> 3 The August has worn against her.
> 4 She does not get up the stairs so eagerly;
>   Yes, she also will turn middle-aged,
>   And the glow of youth that she spread about us
>   As she brought us our muffins
>   Will be spread about us no longer.
>   She also will turn middle-aged. (CSP 127)

The element of decay is best conveyed and generalised in the suggestion that this waitress in the mundane reality of the tea-shop is of uncertain age, not yet middle-aged, but with a certain difficulty in negotiating stairs that is premature if she is still to be described as a girl. All this is clear enough in the context of the poem's ostensible sense, which is summarised in the slow solemnity of the repeated line about middle age. Yet the quite ponderous movement of that sentiment is exploded in a moment of pure bathos: the incursion of the grotesquely ordinary yet unusual sounding word 'muffins' into this observation of the banal. We have already been offered a small hint that the poem is in some sense obtrusive in this scene by the somewhat elegant, elevated, consciously poeticised usage of the third line, which is readily contrasted with the fourth line. The same element of bathos is encapsulated in the word 'muffins' – its sound, its position in the poem and its semantic connotations. This one almost comic word undermines the centrality of the social scene to the poem's process by forcing attention back to the particular qualities of words (and incidentally gives rise to the comic bizarreness of the use of the word 'spread' – spread like butter on the muffins, perhaps?). In its banality 'muffins' also shifts the complacent and sagely nodding observer of the scene, removes him from control and whirls him into a part of language which has the capability of saying something other than what it is due to say. That single word no longer allows the narrative, observing voice to remain detached from the observed scene since the muffins are, explicitly, being brought to him, into his sphere. As even the line arrangement suggests, they quite literally disrupt his banal rumination on a banal scene: thus the poem's final line, its ostensible truth, takes on an entirely different complexion now that it has been repeated. Here, almost, another question mark for the nature of poetic writing, the result of language intruding upon the substance of the scene.

The poem which follows 'The Tea Shop' in *Lustra* is 'Ancient Music':

> Winter is icummen in,
> Lhude sing Goddamm,
> Raineth drop and staineth slop,
> And how the wind doth ramm!
>   Sing: Goddamm.
> Skiddeth bus and sloppeth us,
> An ague hath my ham.
> Freezeth river, turneth liver,
>   Damn you, sing: Goddamm.
> Goddamm, Goddamm, 'tis why I am, Goddamm.
>   So 'gainst the winter's balm
> Sing goddamm, damn, sing Goddamm,
> Sing goddamm, sing goddamm, DAMM. (CSP 127)

This poem, in a manner somewhat related — though perhaps more desired here — to the previous poem, undercuts the observation of a corrupt world (in this case a physically rather than morally corrupt world) by allowing the poem's process to be foregrounded. The poem becomes simply a series of vituperations which, to adopt a distinction made by Barthes,[6] signify very little but rather *signal*, directing the reader not to the poem's production of a meaning but to the very surface of the poem (language's energy and form) and to the fun that might be had there.

The issues raised by the juxtaposition of these poems might be construed as basically questions of language's freedom and play: where the language is apparently at the behest of Pound's central authorial voice, reflecting upon a socially identifiable substance, there are necessary — and unwanted — signs of strain. Pound's concern with the sheer vitality of the poetic line is ever present, but he seems to be in some kind of retreat from the implications of that in many poems — and this becomes especially problematic where that energy proposes itself in contrast to the deadness that a poem like 'The Tea Shop' dallies with. The conflicts in language that arise between this vitality and the distanced feel of a dead civilisation form precisely the topic of 'Mauberley'. There, by and large, language is constrained by a quatrain form but still has much of the freedom which Pound's own metric and diction can establish as a result of his previous flirtation with materiality: that is to say, the very form of the sections of 'Mauberley' betrays the conflicting demands of the old and the new, the dead and the quick as it were. This obvious dialectic is analogous to the wavering between the direct and the allusive, and is apparent in 'Mauberley' at all levels of organisation.

There are two heavily rhetorical and *directly* discursive sections in 'Mauberley': IV ('These fought in any case . . . ') and V ('There died a myriad . . . '). Both of these sections deplore the mortal 'wastage as never before' suffered in the Great War. These two sections are encased by more *allusive* sections: III ('The tea-rose tea-gown . . . ') and 'Yeux Glauques' (CSP 206-209). The latter sections tend towards the bewildering in their swing between direct utterance (as if *in propria persona*)[7] and the arcane or difficult. The lucid finds its almost overdetermined expression in the lines like 'Thin like brook-water, with a vacant gaze' while the difficult is difficult not merely by dint of allusion – we have an extensive body of critical annotation to help us with that – but also by the lack of facility with which verses like

> Still, at the Tate, they teach
> Cophetua to rhapsodize (CSP 209)

trip from the unprepared tongue. The two aspects I am describing never seem to collude and always open up a rhetorical distance between one another.

This seems to be to be the emblem of the whole problematic of Pound's writing: there is an anxious dehiscense between two approaches to poetic practice, between, finally, materiality and substance. And 'Mauberley' is an early and signal display of exactly that problem, as the following stanza from section III might indicate:

> All things are a flowing,
> Sage Heracleitus says;
> But a tawdry cheapness
> Shall outlast our days. (CSP 206)

Here the allusion to Heraclitus (made all the more exclusive by Pound's spelling, and intrusive by its submission to a metrical demand) seems to have little thematic value and only a thin, imposed semantic connection with the two lines that follow (and, indeed, with the poem as a whole). It is especially out of phase with the forthrightness of the second couplet here. Obviously the direct and the allusive are an important structural principle in that they dictate both the poem's organisation of physical material as well as its sense, but at another level they simply represent precisely this paradox in Pound's work, namely that between the demands of and the preoccupation with a quality of language and literary culture and the attraction towards what I have called social space.

There seems, then, to be a continual tension between Pound's conscious artistry and its suitability for dealing with the real. In this context, 'Mauberley' is usually regarded as a reflection on (or of) the frustrated status of poetic sensibility within a hostile milieu. But these tensions seem to me to raise not primarily questions about the way the poet sees himself or is seen in respect to society's ideological positioning of him, but rather more pressingly to suggest questions about how poetic language might have the power to turn the tables on any ideology that holds it in thrall, on the closed specularity of a system which sees poetry as a reflective surface.

Although his work is continually caught up in such questions Pound, by now, is concerned specifically to repress them. It is interesting to see here in 'Mauberley' the first real signs of the reductive drive towards the nominative that takes a hold in Pound's later work so that even the allusiveness of poetry can be reduced and condensed. The cultural references here are naturally (as one is supposed to think, at any rate) given in proper names, in nouns with capital letters so that even the allusive becomes, in some sense, direct. Pound, then, attempts to reduce his cultural world to a series of capital letters just as we saw above that culture itself could be condensed into the capital city or to the centennial (C) thesis. It may be, too, that 'Mauberley' operates as the reduced centre of a cultural polyphony of that sort, and I take the poem as a whole not as a pained and conscious attempt to synthesise the two antithetical tendencies within it, but rather as the parapraxis of a peculiarly sophisticated writing practice that has been twisted into treating objects and vistas unsuited to it. The 'tawdry cheapness' that infests the real social world, and to which the cultural world must relate in Pound's poem, provides an ill-fitting centre for Pound's writing. The upshot of the tension resides in a sort of emptiness in the stanzas like the Heraclitus one, and in similar signs of literary discourse's retreat back into itself. As Donald Davie remarks about this poem, 'differences in tone of voice are precisely what matters far more than the identity of what is said';[8] and beneath these tones of voice I hear a much more schismatic and divisive rumination, one which regards language as a limpid vehicle, a simple communicating mechanism which would be unperverted by the actual act or performance of utterance.

In some sense, then, the greater part of 'Mauberley' 's strength resides in this dialectical movement, a reason for admiring the work. It sets the general principle of contradiction against identity within the actual structuration of the utterance; but this is, finally, a poem which regrets that identity has not survived the process. Contradiction is ultimately a threat, or treated as something accidental or transient which could be rectified or repaired. This, in another context, is the key note to Pound's vehemently restorative politics.

So, in 'Mauberley', we have a poem whose linguistic strategies are capable of laying before the reader the very processes of contradiction in language, while at the same time registering the threatening effect that this might have on traditional literary assumptions. As such, it seems to me admirable in that first gesture but disappointing in the second. It is hardly surprising that, of all Pound's work, this poem finds favour with F.R. Leavis's moral spirit since in that second gesture Pound implicitly tries for the very synthesis, the redemption of contradiction, which might stand outside of process and allow judgement and evaluation to subsist: it attempts a unification of the poem in traditional fashion, enabling Leavis to state approvingly that 'Mauberley does form a whole',[9] a plenitude unthreatened by contradiction.

In contrast to 'Mauberley' and 'The Tea Shop' which both have social subjects as their working matter, many of the *Cantos*, especially from the 'Nuevo Mundo' section, use *textual* particulars in that central role and, indeed, often seem to take their very diction from other texts: the phraseology of 'Canto 31', for example, is drawn without exception and almost verbatim from the letters of Thomas Jefferson and John Adams, which remain as documents of the history of young America. It has been suggested that these American cantos generally were designed 'to tease the reader into looking up sources'.[10] Indeed, one commentator has been sufficiently teased to print 'Canto 31' alongside its source material.[11] But this approach shows itself almost entirely negative and unnecessary since the study of the sources shows quite clearly that the changes Pound imposed upon the order and nature of the original texts are quite minimal, except where his tran-

scriptions act as a sort of précis of given passages — and even there
the actual diction is little altered. Indeed, the extra information that
the reader can cull from the original letters is hardly enlightening. Such
a reading practice seems to do little more than supply the confirmation of a system of values which Pound has already expounded precisely via those originals and which is certainly already apparent in a
reading of the poems themselves.

Analogous to the movement in Pound's earlier verse towards self-
reference, betrayed in the exploitation of the verb 'to sing', for
example, there is a similar movement, marked by the use of simple
verbs of utterance and reference to the act of communication, in 'Canto
31', which begins:

> Tempus loquendi.
> Tempus tacendi.
> 3 Said Mr Jefferson: it wd. have given us
>   time.
> 'modern dress for your statue . . .
> 'I remember having written you while Congress sat at Annapolis,
> 'on water communication between ours and the western country,
> 8 'particularly the information . . . of the plain between
> 'Big Beaver and Cayohoga, which made me hope that a canal
> . . . navigation of Lake Erie and the Ohio. You must have had
> 'occasion of getting better information on this subject
> 12 'and if you have you wd. oblige me
> 'by a communication of it. I consider this canal,
> 'if practicable, as a very important work.'
>   T.J. to General Washington, 1787 (153)

The Malatestan motto which opens this canto is given especial import
by its position next to Jefferson's reported utterance, which in turn
gains a special import. The inversion of the verb in line 3 precisely
throws emphasis on to the saying, the act of communicating as a deliberate choice: wise men can choose properly their time for speaking and
their time for silence, and here in Jefferson we can recognise one of
them. As, generally speaking, in the rest of the canto the position of the
utterance is clearly indicated by the names and dates pertaining to the
correspondence. The utterance itself is thus carefully situated, posi-
tioned, and so brought to the fore as the nature of the concerns in the
letter are continually referred to — typically by the use of the words
'communication' and 'information' which both appear twice in this

short passage. The verb 'to write' also appears here, and so the passage maintains an insistence on the notion of language and writing which is totally in keeping with what we know of Pound's evolving poetics which now views language as the means, simply, of direct and useful transmission — as, in other words, the canal along which information may pass in a regulated and efficient system of exchange for the good of the community. The value of that metaphor to Pound is given very blandly in the claim that this is 'very important work'.

Pound manages in some sense to validate internally his own view of language here: language as the channel for direct communication. He achieves this by the juxtaposition of the opening motif, deriving ultimately from the Bible, with the 'Said Jefferson' inversion. The Malatestan motto arrests the reader with its authoritative air. At first it seems to exhibit the authority of Biblical writing itself since it is in Latin and comes from the Vulgate (perhaps the epitome of encratic language), but later that authority is retracted, imposed upon by Pound's later remark questioning the status of the Scriptures' truth (156). In other words, that authority is first of all used to help Pound's own, and is then undercut and taken over.

So this motto must be seen to act on the canto's system of values as a temporary stay, until Pound's own construction work can stand without it. It simply acts as an internal structuring device: indeed, the phrase has already become privileged simply by its association with the hero of early parts of the *Cantos*, Sigismundo. Now it helps to guarantee the internal cohesion and thus the 'truthfulness' of Pound's own writing. It is probably (and incidentally) accurate to say too that this phrase acts back on to the blank spaces between 'Canto 30' and 'Canto 31': a gap which might have 'suggested the end of an era, the era of the Church's domination'.[12] The gap in history between the Renaissance and the American Revolution is perhaps explained by very dint of being the 'tempus tacendi', but the American Revolution is a watershed in which utterance might be resumed in order to reaffirm the moral ways of the *activa vita*. This is exactly the affirmation that 'Said Jefferson' announces, the re-emergence of man and word from a period of historical silence to reconstruct the proper modes of communication.

And so, at the start of the American cantos, we are thrown straight into the world of Jefferson's documents, just as earlier we were given the documents of Malatesta, his post-bag. The system of moral valency relevant to that world has been established in just these few fine strokes at the very start. And these documents live up to their etymological definition: they will teach, instruct. As verbatim documents from the late eighteenth and early nineteenth centuries they are intended to guarantee the rectitude of certain moral viewpoints: the concerns within them are thus established as privileged contemplations, and must be seen as specific supports to Pound's own moral scheme. The notion of communication, then, is most vital since it acts as a synecdoche for writing itself, for utterance generally; it also gives rise to notions of commerce and thus economy (the latter being aptly defined, since these letters deal with the governance of Pound's homeland, the management of the home). The metaphoric link between writing values and socio-economic values is fundamental to all of Pound's writing. Here, to underscore that link, this canto treats various aspects of the problems facing the new republic, such as freedom, democracy, money, trade, taxes, religion, morality. All the pronouncements stemming from the Jefferson letters have been already validated, endowed with a positive valency, by the simple device I have pointed out in the first three lines.

However obvious it may seem, I should like to stress that the whole of the canto's central core has derived from other people's textual matter, that Pound's *activa vita* is thus necessarily known as some remove. 'Canto 31', with some minor amendments, *substantially* employs a diction which is not Pound's own: the poet is here simply the organiser, the orchestrator of these pieces of language within a form and an order which undertakes to guarantee them a certain moral value. They are the 'external original' that has undergone the purging process of Pound's mind (the editing process) and have now emerged reduced, stripped of all but their 'essential' moral character. Since it is Pound himself who has established what their moral value should be (effectively by interpreting them rather than allowing them any free play), he demonstrates that the necessary consequence of centring his own text is an authoritarian compulsion upon the reader to accept standards of Pound's own devising: he tries to make us believe that these texts he employs could not be read in any other way.

Thus his centring procedure inevitably and clearly precurses the hectoring mode of the later cantos. 'Canto 31' as it stands is a kind of degree zero of Pound's morality in writing since it is composed entirely of supposed guarantees, both of the morality and the writing itself. The reader is left with very few options when dealing with stratagems of this sort (not so uncommon in literature, but seen in extreme form in Pound's work). He can look up the sources and corollary texts while saying aye or nay to the general process — as most readings tend to do; or, I suggest, he can attempt to dismantle the system of values that the text is proposing, and in so doing try to *discredit* the subtle handiwork that Pound displays. Such readings might have as a sort of pleasing adjunct some sense of the comedy that Pound's work specifically represses — the comedy of differing tonalities. The play of discourses in a poem like 'Ancient Music' is clearly designed to be amusing but Pound is more often more serious, and funny only unwittingly. Just as the word 'muffins' brought a sardonic and neutralising light to the solemn tones of the pompous tea-shop observer, so 'Canto 31' includes a certain ludicrous sketch of these literate and solemn old statesmen as they share their concerns without humour: but far from mocking their grandiosity and pomposity Pound's text merely joins with them in repeating it.

(ii) Representation

Drawing the reader into Pound's system of values, refusing to relinquish — only authorise — his earnestness, involves Pound's texts in writing procedures which have to tighten the hold on the reader. If language is to act as this efficient channel it has to plug all its leaks, build strong walls to contain the message as it flows from author to reader. The reader must never be made aware of the artificial nature of what is being offered. In Ford Madox Hueffer's terms, the reader should be 'hypnotized into thinking that he [is] living what he [reads]':[13] that is, he should be hoodwinked into ignoring the mediating characteristics of all our means of communication, into ignoring the materiality of the languages and conventions we live by, and into complicitly accepting the truth of an author's utterance. It is noteworthy that Pound, when talking about the influences of Hulme and Hueffer on Imagism, always preferred to give credit to the latter (who, of course, 'knew about WRITING' (SP 432)) as against Hulme who at least recognised that poetic discourse can 'express reality only in non-real terms'.[14]

This hoodwinking of the reader into implicit belief and trust would constitute precisely a closure, or a tightening, of traditional symbolic systems. Pound deals with this question throughout his work, but perhaps an amusing and signal instance could be dealt with here — in 'Canto 10' where Pound deals with the burning of his hero, Sigismundo, in effigy. Pound's writing procedure here, as I will show, is reminiscent of a moment in history which Marx has analysed.

The sixteenth of April 1848 was one of those moments, according to Marx, when the whole sham of history exposes its own fictional procedures and lays bare the interests that are at work in any given historical scenario. Marx calls the French Provisional Government's attack that day on a legitimate delegation of the proletariat a 'clumsily constructed comedy' which was designed to strengthen the government's political position and provide an excuse for the recall of the armed forces to Paris. The government, by organising a misunderstanding of the workers' assembly, 'had defeated their shadow in a . . . sham fight'.[15] This moment is a heightened symptom of the theatricality of such political manoeuvres as are designed to thwart opposition to the *status quo*, and to strengthen the ideological power of the ruling class. But it is precisely the melodramatic, farcical nature of such ploys that allows Marx the space for his critique: the whole of *The Class Struggles in France, 1848-1850* and *The Eighteenth Brumaire of Louis Bonaparte* are imbued with this theatrical metaphor, leading to Marx's celebrated notion that history repeats itself, first as tragedy, then as farce. For someone like Pound, whose whole aim in writing is to 'tighten the idiom' of traditional practices of communication, and to 'put one's finger on a slip or a momentary inattention', such a lacuna would need to be closed over, so that discourses such as Marx's could no longer have hold. In this respect it is useful to look at this similar moment in Pound's own work, where a critique is made of traditional procedures — not for revolutionary, but for reactionary purposes. By watching Pound pitch his self-proclaiming serious rectitude against the flaws of a system which allows itself to be surprised in its comic theatrical dress, we can notice some centrally important clues to Pound's position within the systems of Western communication.

In 'Canto 10' Pound deals with an instance of such farcical procedures, namely the burning of Sigismundo Malatesta in effigy by Pope Pius II in Rome in 1461. By attacking the assumptions and the political sham which underlie this event, Pound involves himself implicitly in remarking how crucial representational technique is to the whole economy, not only of his own work, but also of traditional modes of communication and organisation. A confirmation of the centrality of the problem might be supplied by the initial executed for 'Canto 10' by Henry Strater.The initial centres around an illustration of the burning, and on either side of that we see written documents: one is a partially rolled scroll, and the other a completely unrolled (and therefore legible) one. I take it that, for my purposes here, the rolled and the unrolled scrolls can be placed in opposition: against the Pope's flawed edict, Pound's clarified edict (see Figure II).[16]

The facts of the burning are given to the reader by a straightforward

Figure II

ND the poor devils dying of cold, outside Sorano,
And from the other side, from inside the château,
Orsini, Count Pitigliano, on the 17th of November:
" Siggy, darlint, wd. you not stop making war on insensible
" objects, such as trees and domestic vines, that have no
" means to hit back ... but if you will hire yourself out to
" a commune (Siena) which you ought rather to rule than
" serve ..."
              which with Trachulo's damn'd epistle ...
And what of it *any*how? a man with a ten acre lot,
Pitigliano ..... a lump of tufa,
              And S. had got back their horses
And the poor devils dying of cold ...

transcription into the canto from Pound's own reading experience:

INTEREA PRO GRADIBUS BASILICAE S. PIETRI EX ARIDA
MATERIA INGENS PYRA EXTRUITUR IN CUJUS SUMMITATE
IMAGO SIGISMUNDI COLLOCATUR HOMINIS LINEAMENTA,
ET VESTIMENTI MODUM ADEO PROPRIE REDDENS, UT
VERA MAGIS PERSONA, QUAM IMAGO VIDERETUR; NE
QUEM TAMEN IMAGO FALLERET, ET SCRIPTURA EX ORE
PRODIIT, QUAE DICERET: SIGISMUNDUS HIC EGO SUM
MALATESTA, FILIUS PANDULPHI, REX PRODITORUM, DEO
ATQUE HOMINIBUS INFESTUS, SACRI CENSURA SENATUS
IGNI DAMNATUS; SCRIPTURUM MULTI LEGERUNT. DEINDE
ASTANTE POPULO, IGNI IMMISSO, ET PYRA SIMULACRUM
REPENTE FLAGRAVIT. (Com. Pio II. Liv. VII, p. 85, Yriarte,
p. 288)

Pound's citing of the reference (Emile Yriarte's biography of Sigismundo, *Un Condottierre au XVe Siecle*, published in 1882), here has
the effect of locating his own act of reading in what we might call,
for want of a better term, a scholarly tradition. In doing this he bolsters

the authority of his own magisterial role in the pointing out, or in arranging (for) the significance of Yriarte's text within his own. Implicitly the reader is assumed to be part of a certain and established signifying practice: the author, source of truth, hands to the reader the *traditional* role of consumer of that truth.

The transcription of Pius's commentary, now at two removes from its original context, becomes more than usually interesting when we consider that it too deals with a sort of magisterially determined system of meaning. The Pope has originally established an explicitly false and empty signifier in this effigy of Malatesta which is designed to replace a reality which is not, in fact, available to be represented. Pius is here indulging in that most respectable of traditional aesthetic modes, namely imitation, or copying from nature. Signally, however, he offers his construct to the reading public as a falsity: the representamen of the effigy in Pius's act of signification is specifically given to the people to be read ('ET SCRIPTURA EX ORE PRODIIT . . . '), and the reason for that writing is to prevent the public from being deceived ('NE QUEM TAMEN IMAGO FALLERET . . . '). What happens here is paradoxical: Pius copies nature by means of his effigy (having, according to Pound, gone to great expense to produce the convincing likeness), and yet this signifier blatantly denies its own status as purveyor of truth, disclaims its own value. Indeed, the falsity of the whole enterprise is emphasised by the fact that the burning took place at several different spots in Rome at the same time.[17]

To Pound, of course, the whole affair appears as a hopelessly naive and fictitious event, and a subject merely for mockery: in its farcical theatricality it is a demonstration of the fallen condition of classical representational discourse (which, in some sense, Pound's whole career was devoted to remedying). Since the falsity of Pius's representation is perfectly overt, Pound with his 'presentative' method feels capable of placing the incident in this canto in the blandest manner – that is, by simply copying it down. This internal juxtaposition allows the direct contrasting of traditional representative method with the new Poundian presentative method, developed by Imagism. It is a comparison evidently designed to do damage to the former.

And yet the difference in the representational and presentational modes of discourse are not so much apart as Pound would like us to believe: they represent, in fact, merely differences in technique rather than in epistemology. Indeed, Pound, while never openly avowing it, has done exactly the same as Pius (who may at least be given credit for recognising the lie in this 'undignified piece of tomfoolery').[18] Pound too has constructed an image of Malatesta which he places on top of (or which rises out of) the vast pile of arid material formed by the historical documents which inform the canto ('EX ARIDA MATERIA INGENS PYRA EXTRUITUR IN CUJUS SUMMITATE IMAGO SIGISMUNDI . . . '). The difference between Pound and Pius is simply one of degree, and is located in the *value* assigned to the constructed image. This value is not constituted upon anything other than an act of will: Pound's strategy is to hand his image of Sigismundo to the reader by the rhetoric of such phrases as 'our brother' which align him, Pound and the reader against the abuse he suffers from the clerics. Just as Pound's presentation of Pius in this canto is alien in technique to Pius's representation of Sigismundo, so Pound's rhetoric against Pius is alien to the rhetoric brought against Sigismundo. Pound merely and easily assumes that his own construction of 'our brother', extracted from documents which are implicitly credited with more 'truth' than the reality from which the Papacy drew its image, is the active and reliable one: thus, these documents are given as the proper representatives of truth, as are other documents throughout the *Cantos*, from Jefferson's letters to K'ang Hsi's *Sacred Edict*. This assumption on Pound's part, and the role it plays in the signifying process, is nothing like the antidote or correction to traditional poetics that Pound imagines it to be: it is just an extreme version of representation in which Pound attempts to restore the signifier to its signified; he tries to elide the material gap in order to restore faith and confidence in the *word* as an instrument in the revelation of reality.

Traditionally, as the burning illustrates, representation entails the erection of a form whose corresponding reality is actually elsewhere; any such form lives in a paradox since it is, once constructed, *actually imaginary*. Pound's representational technique further distances this form by deriving it from some other representations – that is, from documents – and then proceeds simply to dictate that form's place in a peculiar system of values which the reader is called upon to trust without question (since that system has the authority of documents, things designed to teach, behind it). In other words, Pound's Malatesta is a fiction of a fiction, installed as truth, validating the present in the name of the past and satisfying Pound's deeply nostalgic desire for the restoration of that past.

The actual effigy burned by Pius points not only to the essentially false but to the decisive *funerary* nature of representation. Pound's method, and its choice of subject in some of the earlier cantos, emphasises the aptness of this adjective. Sigismundo's achievements are in the building of the Tempio at Rimini as a monument to his dead mistress Isotta; the Tempio itself then becomes a sort of empty signifier to take her place, and is all the more pathetic in its grandiloquence. At best it remains a testament to the energy expended, the cost incurred, in the instruction of classical representations out of an inability to recognise and accept that the signified cannot be recalled, only – and unsatisfactorily – replaced. The nature of the drives that operate here and in the similarity between Pound and his antagonist is underlined by Pound's penchant for the monumental in his own work: as examples one might point out the city plaque and the words 'These words I read on a pyramid . . . ' (the pyramid being the epitome of the grandiose signifier enshrining a dead or empty core) in 'Canto 34'; or similarly the monument of the eulogy to Van Buren at the end of 'Canto 37'.

It is something of an irony, then, that it should be exactly this funerary aspect of representation, its essentially morbid and fictional nature, which moves Pound to a condemnation of the Pope's practices. Just as the empty signifier in the effigy incident is attacked by Pound, so is any other utterance or gesture which apears to establish signifiers remote from any pragmatically realisable referent. One thinks of Dido hugging Sicheus' corpse in 'Canto 7' or the installation of the murdered Ignez da Castro on the Spanish throne in 'Canto 30'. In this light we might see the persistent references in the earlier cantos (radiating especially from 'Canto 7') to the outer casings of death as Pound's attack on what he sees as the emptiness of the signifier in traditional representation. There is a dialectical commerce between that emptiness and the vigour of Pound's own process of writing. In 'Canto 7' the image of life and energy resides in the vision of Nicea, the poet's privately owned fantasy: 'We alone have being' (26). This vision is set against the illusory and life-denying signifiers that persist in Pound's time, a time when language has fallen to such a state that 'Words [are] like the locust shells, moved by no inner being,' there exists a 'dryness calling for death' and men are just 'thin husks' within a cultural environment reduced to a shell, 'a sham' (26/7). Yet what one critic has called the 'near comedy of the handling'[19] in this Nicea image helps to undercut the simple juxtaposition of the quick and the dead. Pound's private image of life is threatened by his own incongruously comic, theatrical imagery, and by the stilted preciousness of his diction:

> . . . all that day
> Nicea moved before me
> And the cold grey air troubled her not

> For all her naked beauty, bit not the tropic skin,
> And the long slender feet lit on the curb's marge
> And her moving height went before me,
>> We alone have being. (26)

It is exactly where such moments of comedy can be read that Pound is most vulnerable, when the interests that are at work in his poetics again become observable. Indeed, Pound's whole project of excising slips and inattentions in traditional discourse comes up against his inability to remove them from his own. Although he sees very clearly how such moments can threaten Pius's discourse, he appears not to remark the opening of the theatrical scene within his own work. Consequently, his desire to repress the very mechanisms of representation in language — that is, his desire to repress the gap between signifier and signified so that he can obtain mastery over language — situates him under the same spotlight in which someone like Mussolini, another seeker of total mastery, can be seen as a comic figure. In attacking Pius's discourse Pound does not wish to contain its mastery of the real, but rather hide the opening, the theatrical flaw which leaves the whole enterprise open to hostile questioning: Pound, then, attacks not the stratagem itself or its epistemology, but its failure to defend and camouflage itself.

The crucial factor here is that moment of substitution in language when the signifier replaces the signified. Pius's message allows us publicly to view that moment, but Pound, far from trying to ensure that it deceives nobody ('NE QUEM TAMEN FALLERET . . . '), wishes it to become, as in Hueffer's style, a secret occurrence. But readers can have their own openings on to that secret exchange. The moments when authorial control is rebelled against, or is superseded, can open up the conventionally funerary elements of the representational process which encourage the confusion of the 'live' and present signifier with the absent and 'dead' signified.

In Pound this confusion, a version of Warburg's *Denkraumverlust*,[20] wishes to clear the air from around the moment of substitution and so insulate traditional practices from the subverting demands of language itself; it is a stratagem that has entirely to do with control. The authoritarian imposition that Pound goes in for is symptomatised in his penchant for the monumental that I spoke of above. The funerary mode of representation expresses itself easily in the monumental or statuary procedures that Pound adopts — it is not for nothing that the topic of sculpture is raised so often in discussions of Pound. Pound wishes to rectify the absence of the signified by the erection of a certain solidity in its place. And, of course, this substitution is of immense import. To put it in social terms, the event that immediately (and silently) occurs after a man's death is the handing on of his rights and property to his heir, the next proprietor. This substitution of one man for another is intended to confirm the tradition: the heir is given his position in society. Here, the statuary is the statutory, endorsed by law and legal requirement, its object being to fix individuals in a given position and thus facilitate the functions and modes of exchange upon which Western society is predicated. In order that commodities may enter into their required relations and so that their proprietors can easily recognise each other as such, the juridical relationships between people (which Marx so often talks about) have to be affirmed.

It is certainly no accident that throughout his life Pound maintained more than a passing interest in right-wing economic systems which aimed for the increased efficiency of such a fixed state of socio-economic identifications, since the exchange and transmission of Pound's own commodity as poet — namely meaning — is based traditionally upon an analogous power of substitution. The upholding of a particular social form is intimately connected with the efficiency of the process whereby precise meaning is established and handed on (for Althusser, of course, all ideology is a *representation* of social relations). Precisely in his concern for the process of the transmission of fixed meanings Pound demonstrates his essential authoritarianism. He merely requires that the wholly traditional system, which has so many gaps and flaws, should cover itself up, remove itself from the scene of debate and be unafraid to exist in its proper totalitarian form — that, in other words, it should stop its ham-acting.

3 TOWARDS VERACITY

Pound's position as he launches into the fourth and fifth decades of the *Cantos* is that of an evangelical priest, intent upon using his language and intuitions into history and economics as weapons in the struggle to reinstate a system of values whose tradition has somewhat failed or been despised by the ignorance of successive generations. The sacerdotal role, marked on the title page of *Lustra*, takes its keynote from the implicit theology of Imagism — May Sinclair had described the Imagists as 'Catholic; they believe in Transubstantiation. For them the bread and wine *are* the body and the blood.'[1] Pound's theology is so rigidly and committedly 'catholic' that it needs to combat and ridicule the frailities of actually existing institutions, as epitomised by his prosecution of Pope Pius II's procedures. Pound presents, then, a sort of dissidence, relying upon the idea that it is there where the 'religion' is rooted that it is most to be venerated, where it is most correct. In the *Cantos* he is attempting to proffer the *documentary* ground in which the roots may again take hold.

This chosen role is assumed with increasing enthusiasm in the American cantos and the Leopoldine Reform cantos, shaping a 'steady crescendo of raucous arrogance'[2] reaching its climax in the fascistic speeches made for Radio Rome during the war years. Those speeches mark the final point of what Wyndham Lewis has called Pound's transition 'from soft to hard'[3] — precisely, the move from the melopoeia of the early poems to the issuing of priestly directives in the later work. We are not, let it be said, dealing with a Rilke-type priest, wrapped in the mysterium and uttering oracles from within; or, indeed, with the demotic, worker-priest that is the reputation of Carlos Williams; rather, Pound acts as the paternal Moses-figure, a law-giver who is proprietor to a certain truth and morality which must be made available (monumentally) to the erring masses.

Even after the forced abandonment of some of his sacerdotal enthusiasm (after his humiliation in the DTC camp at Pisa, that is), Pound never quite quits this priestly role. The ritual burning of olibanum that was necessary before Pound would converse at St Elizabeths[4] is less the symptom of a man dubbed insane than the vestige of this pontifical trait and part of the personality (the celebrated and various personae having been dropped along with the possibilities of autonomous poetic language) of this man who is claimed by his disciples to be writing 'one of the greatest religious poems of recent centuries'.[5]

The great theophanic revelation to which Pound lends the maieutic power of his writing is that of the ultimate social order upheld by the moral proprieties that efficient communication fosters. This *telos* is given the mantle of several different metaphors within the *Cantos*: the later parts of the poem assume especially the metaphor of a 'great ball of crystal' (795), the image of cohesion and solidity, clarity and durability. This is the culminating expression in the *Cantos* of the 'forma' that Donald Davie has dealt with at length.[6] Davie has noted the variable recurrence in the poem of images of stone, marble, glass and crystal, water and so on. These notions, derived from Adrian Stokes' emphasis on the kinship of marble and water,[7] are corroborated by a certain connection of Jung's: there, the body ' is carbon . . . also it is well known that the diamond is a carbon crystal. Carbon is black — coal, graphite — but the diamond is purest water.'[8] This formula's metonymic connections may be used to underscore Pound's thematics: not only does it position the blackness of historical ignorance from which the crystal is supposed to arrive in Pound's poem, but in its connection about the body it produces the suggestive possibility of the body itself becoming the crystal, and so it presages the metamorphosis of the ball of crystal into 'That great acorn of light bulging outward' (755) in almost comic suggestion of the glans of the penis (and, of course, 'We *flop* if we cannot maintain the awareness' (557) of the revealed truth).

Even if my suggestion might appear fanciful, it none the less can shed some light on the way in which the path of revelatory experience seems to be illuminated for Pound himself. In its sexual suggestion it helps explain the frequent preparatory appearance of female godheads in the poem, goddesses who emerge from the chaos of particulars to become assistants in the poet's drive towards light and enlightenment. The feminine apparition is never the form of the revelation itself but merely a dispensable sign on the way to it. This is a theme that has been running through Pound's work from the very beginning: the visitation by 'the eyes of this dead lady' (CSP 84), for example, or the appearance of Francesca (CSP 50), the beauty of the woman in the aptly titled 'Apparuit' (CSP 80), and the female eyes preserved by Burne-Jones' drawings mentioned in 'Mauberley' (CSP 209) are all forebears of the goddesses who announce the coming of the 'forma' in the *Cantos*. The visit of Aphrodite is, of course, not 'the full Εἰδὼς' (520), not the crystal itself but simply the encouragement towards it. Such a role characterises Elizabeth Tudor in her instigation of Sir Francis

Drake:

> Miss Tudor moved them with galleons
> from deep eye, versus armada
> from the green deep
>   he saw it,
> in the green deep of an eye. (611)

In this passage the watery base of the body is again played upon: the male adventurer and discoverer is influenced by an urging light which is similar to that which inhabits the crystal, but which is not it. The female is then seen as the force which inspires a man on his natural path towards the light; she employs compassion and sympathy, necessary to comfort him in his difficult and dangerous task of achieving the light of proper social ordinance. It is ' . . . "our job to build light" said Ocellus' (684), but it is clearly not the woman's job.

Woman's tied role in the construction of social perfection is dealt with at length in the early cantos and also, in a way in which women seem to benefit from Pound's supposed new humility, in the Pisan cantos. It must be remembered that the qualities which found the proper social order according to Pound and his followers[9] all add up to a form of love. One of Pound's own statements of the relation between love and social order can be found in his translation of Cavalcanti's 'Donna mi Prega' in 'Canto 36'. This translation has been described as impenetrable and as perhaps earning its place in the *Cantos* by very dint of that impenetrability.[10] It seems to me that the translation is to some extent simply a remnant of Pound's former delight in pure melopoeia, in the verbal music which can be achieved by giving the materials of writing priority over message. Indeed, the qualities as utterance that this canzon has are, as we might expect, emphasised by Pound's old stratagem of reference to the enunciatory act: 'I speak in season . . . I speak to the present knowers . . . 'tis felt, I say' (177/8). Such references culminate in the little 'Go, song' envoi (179). These reflexive elements aside, the canzon nevertheless manages to articulate several of the beams of Pound's poetic architectonics. This poem is, after all, uttered from the pontifical bivouac that the uninitiated cannot penetrate:

> Wherefore I speak to the present knowers
> Having no hope that low-hearted
>   Can bring sight to such reason

> Be there not natural demonstration
> I have no will to try proof-bringing. (177)

The role of the woman — the partner, after all, in love — seems to be a direct function of that secret locus of utterance. In the canzon it is the woman who, understanding not, asks the poet to explain about love. And she is immediately elided from the discussion which constitutes the answer to her question. The case is even clearer in the original Italian where the starting word 'Donna . . . ' is the woman's only mention. As a telling symptom of this elision of the female it is interesting to note that in his earlier translation of this poem Pound actually uses the words 'her face', but these are signally omitted from the version in 'Canto 36'.[11] We are to understand, of course, that disputation is man's business; the very act of utterance and the performance of intellectual understanding are deliberately removed from woman's grasp:

> You are tender as a marshmallow, my Love,
> I cannot use you as a fulcrum. (632)

So in this piece of work the woman has a strictly delimited role. She is, in an important sense, the poem's base and its impulse, but after bestowing the gift of inspiration on the male she is to appear no more: after all, it is the Drakes and Pounds of this world who actually go out and do things. Here, indeed, Pound is quite content to know nothing of the identity of Cavalcanti's inspiration in his introduction to his translations. In this instance, as generally, by regarding the woman as of only provisional interest Pound underlines his basically patriarchal stance. Here he hardly allows a later apologist for his anti-feminism, J.J. Wilhelm, the argument that the troubadours' ladies 'are raised up a step by being the sources of much of their inspiration'. Although Wilhelm claims that to Pound female energy 'is both stimulating and delightful',[12] a poem such as 'Shop Girl' would indicate how he can consider it only initially diverting, useful 'for a moment' before his staunchly literary utterance can take control:

> For a moment she rested against me
> Like a swallow half blown to the wall,
> And they talk of Swinburne's women,
> And the shepherdess meeting with Guido.
> And the harlots of Baudelaire. (CSP 123)

That neglect of the feminine, then, has everything to do with the establishment of the desired Poundian civics, even though that system appeals to a notion of love for describing itself and advertising its value. The Poundian teleology works from a base in nature towards the manifestation of a natural social and linguistic order: the definitive division of the sexes, and the assignation of strict roles to each of them, is integrally part of that teleology. The clarification of the feminine role as inspiration and base, set against the masculine role of ordering and elaboration, comes when Pound begins to use a version of Stokes' material distinction between carving and modelling in sculpture.

In making his distinction Stokes claims that 'Man, in his male aspect, is the cultivator or carver of woman who, in her female aspect, moulds her products as does the earth.'[13] Although Stokes goes on to inform us that in the production of art the two have to be to a certain extent interdependent, the whole burden of his treatise *The Stones of Rimini* is to install an art which elevates the masculine carving ideal to a position of pre-eminence. In other words, a damage is done, a sexual *parti pris* firmly taken. Stokes' elaborations of his idea sound a very definite Poundian moral note: talking of Agostino's work in the temple at Rimini, Stokes imagines that 'the stone block is female, the plastic figures that emerge from it on Agostino's reliefs are her children, the proof of the carver's love for the stone.'[14] This sort of expression attaches to all of Pound's praise for artists who manifest a special kind of almost mystical attachment to their materials like, for example, Henri Gaudier-Brzeska, whose regard for 'the nature of the medium, of both the tools and the actual matter' (GB 10) vindicates and characterises his inevitably phallic 'urge to physical activity' (GB 39). It should be remembered that it was Gaudier who, in a reciprocating gesture of vindication, carved the famous hieratic head of Ezra Pound.

Stokes views the sexual action performed by the artist upon his material as productive of the best sort of art. It is the 'profundity of such communion'[15] that he finds so appealing. Using such terms he is aligning himself very closely with Pound's sacerdotal streak and to the vocabulary that pervades Pound studies. That mystical communion of male and female forces, the male on top, is precisely what Pound is getting at in 'Canto 36' with its 'sacrum, sacrum inluminatio coitu' (180), or later with his 'in coitu inluminatio' (435).

The sacred quality of the male and female roles as Pound understands them and as they are expounded in Stokes' early writings, and as they are further elaborated in Pound's Cavalcanti connection, may be said to guarantee the function of phallic power. The ultimate communion with the great clarity (which can be seen as the acorn, the head of the penis) is the object of 'man's phallic heart' (697), of his aim as it proceeds along the lines of the tensile light which illumines the proper structure of social connections. The female principle is elided along the way, even though it is of indispensable help as inspiration and charitable compassion. The stone likewise loses its specificity as the active male carves it, or inseminates it to reveal its proper form; the female inspiration to song is forgotten in the drive towards the light of male understanding and creativity. In such a scheme of things the female role is amenable, made to appear significant only through the activity of masculinity as it encroaches upon passivity. Even such a crude assignation of active and passive roles to the male and female is already totally a question of *tradition* and convention, as Freud has pointed out.[16]

This obtrusive phallocentric drive in Pound's work is exceedingly difficult to miss. I may well be labouring the point, but it actually appears that some reactions to Pound and his work either disregard it or welcome it. A telegram to the editors of *Paideuma* from Sheri Martinelli, one of Pound's lovers, affirms a blind faith in 'MY DEAREST & BEST & MOST BELOVED TEACHER'. Martinelli stiffens her message with a dose of sexism and racism, no doubt learnt from her master, when she demands 'WHAT MANNER OF WHITE MALE IS THIS . . . ' who dares dismiss Pound and Pound studies out of hand;[17] Hilda Doolittle, as her memoir of Pound, *An End to Torment*, demonstrates, spent many years awestruck and terrified by Pound's image and influence before the very writing of the memoir exorcised him;[18] among the critics, J.J. Wilhelm blandly denies that the *Cantos* can give an overall impression of anti-feminism;[19] C. David Heymann follows Dorothy Pound's example of 'not complaining, merely relating a cold fact' when having to deal with Pound's callous elision of Dorothy from his life in later years;[20] Christine Brooke-Rose, although recognising the oppressive male/female split between the 'iconoclastic rough and tumble' male and the passive, receptive female, qualifies and glosses over that attitude by claiming that these are 'non-antagonistic pairs' and that the female, despite Pound's denigration and patronising of her, acts as the unwobbling pivot in the organisation of the *Cantos.*[21]

Donald Davie, without remarking much on the phallocentric mode, has linked the Stokesian expression of the matter specifically with 'Canto 47' by importing the analogy between masculine carving of the block and the ploughing of the earth. His terms come extremely close to the phrases of Stokes that I quoted above. It seems to me that 'Canto

47' is an excellent place to view both Pound and his critics at work. Not only does this canto include in its very structure a network expressing Pound's notion of the design of nature and natural regeneration in relation to the female, but it is also a clear example of how Pound's language moves along lines that are dictated by the great acorn itself. It is further of exemplary interest by force of the high esteem in which it is held by various critics. In exposing some of this canto's underlying assumptions about language and human activity, I hope to make an implicit point about the traditional Poundian criticism which can regard this work as an example of 'Pound at his best'[22] or as one of his 'peaks of poetic achievement'.[23]

There seems to me to exist a certain type of reading stratagem lying behind the sort of judgements I have just mentioned. This is a stratagem which confines its attention to, first of all, isolating, and then collating, thematic strands in the text. What would emerge from such a reading here is Pound's faith in the sufficiency of natural cyclical process for the generation of value and goodness. This is Pound's originary and central assumption from which he proceeds to his special view of history, a view consisting in setting, on the one hand, those manifestations of human culture which are desirable and beneficial, because mimetic of natural growth and abundance, against those, on the other hand, which are corrupt and decadent in having denied or abrogated that process. On the page, Pound's view is presented as a set of juxtaposed exempla — though not necessarily in a balanced juxtaposition since Pound allows the emphasis to wander from one side to the other. These exempla are mediated by a certain rhetorical lyricism which, in its especially connotative vocabulary, acts to underline the importance of the natural world to the philosophy of value that is being proposed.

Of course, what I have just said acts as a simplistic paraphrase of the sort of critical work most usually done on this and other cantos. Efficient though that work often is, it does seem (as may appear from my brief description of it) to maintain a coalescence or a certain faith with Pound's epistemology. As Pound has interlocked his perceptions along the line of certain themes, so the critics expect to be able to unlock the full meaning. J.J. Wilhelm has argued that this unlocking procedure is particularly apposite in the case of 'Canto 90', where the canto's Latin epigraph is translated right at the end of the poem. These translated lines, according to Wilhelm, 'now loosen the Latin locked in as the epigraph for the canto' and the passage of our reading across the text is led to the actuality of the full, translated clarity of Pound's meaning. It might, however, equally well be argued that the epigraph and its translation literally close up the canto at both ends and thus lock in more than anything else. If I insist on this small distinction it is because it is emblematic of my view that the simple confidence in scholarship's ability (and there is no shortage of traditional scholarly attention paid to Pound's work) to disentangle Pound's veritable meaning is restrictive, confining itself to the project of this translating of Pound's intention.[24]

The area of themes charted by most critics in writing like 'Canto 47' can demonstrate their (and Pound's) propensity for reducing language to fixed meanings within the control of the author. It is important to see how the features of this canto all work by establishing common denominators amongst very different poetic resources and by distilling these to areas of identity. This is a process of reduction: the critics keenly follow Pound's lead in this. One of the most notable features of 'Canto 47' is its juxtaposition of different texts, or documents, which are representative of different historical moments. There is a version of Bion's 'Lament for Adonis', a piece of Homer's *Odyssey*, and an extract from Hesiod. These texts clearly are demarcated within the canto's arrangement, but they are joined by association: one of the links, for example, between Odysseus and Adonis is made by the fact that they were both called to the underworld as a prelude to the reaching of their proper goals, Penelope and Venus respectively. That link is made all the more explicit by the appearance of Persephone within the Homer translation. There is also an implicit metaphorical link between the darkness of Hell and the darkness of Circe's intent in her encounter with Odysseus. The *Odyssey* and the Bion text are then linked to the Hesiod by their associated interest in the masculine activities of mensuration and the proper counting of the stars — rationality, in short; the Pleiades, Odysseus' stellar guide in the shape of a plough, provide the link with ploughing and deploy a parallel between the agrarian calendar and cycles of the seasons. Obviously there exist more than just these few links in this canto, but these should suffice to establish that the juxtaposed texts are in fact fused together by the sort of association that is brought about by metonymy.

Distinct from these written texts, this canto also contains what might be called oral texts — myths which come down to us as a fusion of several cultural sources and whose effect is achieved in despite of the differences in those sources. For example, Tammuz and Adonis are proper names attached to the myth of seasonal death and regeneration embodied in a god, and their use here indicates a common attachment to such a myth. Clearly, it is this dispensation of similarity which allows the compilers of the *Annotated Index to the Cantos* to then refer to Tammuz and Adonis as 'equivalent'.[25] Such a description chooses to ignore the differences in cultural and temporal provenance which are also properly attachable to these names. The result is a damage done to temporal specificity, arising from an emphasis upon deliberately selected common denominators rather than on equally possible and important distinctions. Pound is here constructing juxtapositions which simply become reductions.

The two quite broadly similar features that have so far been described at work in this canto go towards structuring the poem by supplying a context for the particular metonymic chains that run through it informing its meaning. The simplest movement of the canto — that is, its linear passage from beginning to end — may be said to generate most obviously the following chain:

(1) sexual adventure inspires the voyage to hell and thus to knowledge;
(2) emergence from Hell into knowledge;
(3) Hell as woman (darkness and irrationality) with the feminine in opposition to phallic power;
(4) sexual activity as intrinsic to natural process, necessarily entailing growth and reproduction; partaking of sex means partaking of knowledge;
(5) knowledge of natural process (located by imagery of light and revelation) institutes human culture and its demands and structures.

It is, most simply, the poem's sequential growth that dictates the parameters for the selection of this particular set of connections: clearly, other chains are equally evident and possible apart from those that are derived from linear progression. Various combinations of similar metonymic connections may be constructed by considering the relationships in Pound's writing between any of the following terms (which are themselves just a shorthand for various longer strands):

darkness; light; coition (male and female imagery); growth; seasonal cyclism; voyaging (e.g. to the underworld); knowledge; culture; religious institutions; social laws; etc.

It becomes evident from this crude list that the primary poetic strategy of this canto is one of metonymy. This enjoins, of course, the fact that

Pound's selection of various particulars to furnish his poetic strands is of less intrinsic importance than the simple fact of their being woven together: metonymy is the trope of the syntagmatic axis of language. So it becomes true to say, as Pound indeed does say, that in the *Cantos* 'a thing *is* what it does'[26] — its qualities as part of the axis of contiguity in the signifying chain are more prevalent than its role in the axis of selection.

Herbert Schneidau has recognised this metonymic principle at work in Pound's writing: he constructs his article 'Wisdom Past Metaphor' around Jakobson's distinction between the metaphorical and the metonymic axes of language.[27] His initial *aperçu* of Pound's inclination towards the metonymic axis leads him to the conclusion that the most 'powerful principle' in the poem is what he calls 'contexture', a mode of concern which emphasises contiguity, or metonymy. But as a simple example of 'contexture' Schneidau gives the 'choosing of a word because of its rhyme instead of its "sense" ' — this is clearly the mode that I am claiming Pound is engaged in repressing by this stage of his career. Schneidau's feelings about the consequences of Pound's bias seem not to take into account the unease that the Pound of the *Cantos* appears to feel about precisely those contextual decisions, or the fact that Pound uses metonymy to establish, as I have shown, 'la simple réunion des traits choisis à la seule fin d'appareiller leur différence'.[28]

The above words are those of Jacques Lacan and it is to him that it might be profitable to turn in order to help clarify the paradox about Pound's use of metaphor and metonymy that emerges from Schneidau's account. In Lacan's work we find a specific reading of Jakobson's fundamental distinction, related to Freudian theory.[29] Lacan follows Jakobson by suggesting that metaphor, which superimposes one signifier over another, is equivalent to Freud's notion of condensation; and metonymy, with its word to word movement, is connected with Freud's displacement. For Freud, displacement and condensation are fundamental tropes in the operation of the unconscious and Lacan is thereby authorised to formulate his celebrated statement that the unconscious is structured as a language. The linguistic movement of metonymy seems to Lacan actually to found human desire since, in its displacement from signifier to signifier (that is, in a movement which does not realise the signified), it 'permits the elision through which the signifier installs lack of being in the object relation, by employing the value of reference-back of the signification in order to invest it with the desire that is aimed at the lack which [desire] supports'.[30] Thus the individual subject and language itself are articulated upon that lack which it is the function of metonymic process to cross continually. Human desire subsists upon the metonymic process in its *mot à mot* motion, and desire can be then called up for the human subject by the relation of signifiers in a metonymic chain.

Desire is endless. Its movement in language is based on the very lack that Freud and Lacan see as being produced by the castration anxiety. Lacan tells us that desire is seen in action 'reproduisant la relation du sujet à l'objet perdu'.[31] So Pound's preference for the metonymic pole of language, the search for which takes place, according to Schneidau, beyond conventional metaphorical structure, can be taken as an expression of his relation to the lost object. What I have to say about the *Cantos* expects to show that Pound is attempting to halt the process of signification at the very point where anxiety about that lack is presented and where desire disrupts again the certainty about language that Pound spent his career trying to foster. The halting of the metonymic chain at safe points is effected under the aegis of conventional masculinity, under the symbolic power of the phallus.

Returning to Schneidau we can take up the argument again. His is the language of the typical Poundian critic, shadowing the humanistic assumptions and attitudes of Pound himself. He seems to take for granted that Pound's poetry and its methodology (which he is, after all, claiming to be primarily metonymic) seek the 'magnification of difference. But it can also trace the overlay of patterns of continuity'.[32] It is here that we might notice a sort of restatement of Pound's own confusions: language is asked to do two things at once which are contradictory; and so, as Pound's so-called metonymic method is put into action, it begins to be treated as if it were metaphoric. Instead of there existing a continual chain of displaced meanings, metaphorical process interrupts. Metaphor involves the substitution of one signifier for another so that there remains a hidden signifier elided by another. The hidden signifier falls to the rank of the signified. The introduction of fixity into the metonymic process, halting its indefinite and floating chain, attempts to deny desire and establish a solidity of meaning – and thus a security for the speaking subject. This, of course, is a process analogous to what we saw in the 'Donna mi Prega' translation where the female, the cipher of desire as it were, is elided in favour of a second signifier – literarity, which guarantees the realm of masculinity.

There is an equation to be made between fixed meaning and masculine knowledge throughout Pound's work. Extrapolating from his imagery in 'Canto 47' and elsewhere about the dissemination of natural

seed and its link with the dissemination of knowledge, or semantic seed
(a link which is corroborated by English etymology,of course), the primary signifer which emerges is the Lacanian lost object, the phallus.
In this canto, indeed, the phallus is immediately palpable, not only in
the explicit context of sexual generation and union ('So light is thy
weight on Tellus . . . Hast'ou a deeper planting . . . Hast thou entered
more deeply the mountain') but also in the multivalency of other areas
of the text: 'Io! Io!' might be taken as a graphic representation of male
genitalia; the many 'Hast'ou' or 'Hast thou' refrains might be taken to
transform phonologically to *hasta*, a spear; 'Two oxen are yoked for
plowing' includes a sexual innuendo within its agrarian specificity; 'The
stars fall from the olive branch' clearly alludes to male ejaculation. In
other words, senses other than those which patently contribute to the
canto's discursive content concur parapractically in demonstrating the
presence of the phallus.

Such phallocentrism might have major and distressing implications
for readers of this text: these Poundian concerns follow on from, or
underlie, a simplistic societal view of the female as necessarily passive
until activated by the male – a view which in revindicating the phallus's
power to control defends the holder against the threat of castration and
the realisation of lack. The view is further endorsed in this canto by
appeal to the naturalness of that condition since it is in the act of
planting, the injection of seed, that the natural vegetative cycle is
upheld. In this and other related ways Pound's text assumes and
endorses patriarchal structures in society and culture. Indeed, Pound's
whole sense of culture derives directly from the assertion of the phallus
as it halts metonymic flow and establishes a fixity of meaning and a
return to the signified. These are traditional stratagems – quite literally so, since they are designed to facilitate the handing on of meaning
from author to reader, from father to son.

Pound's traditionalism in this respect becomes apparent in his use of
the *Odyssey*. The manner of his strategy amounts to a direct transmission of the phallocentrism in Homer's text into his own – right, as it
were, from the very roots of Western culture into the heart of what
goes by the name of modernism.We find in Homer[33] that Hermes, 'god
of the golden wand', warns Odysseus to 'draw your sword' and rush at
Circe in order to make her 'shrink from you in terror and invite you to
her bed'; as if that peculiar causality did not say enough about the
workings of traditional masculinity, Hermes goes on to warn Odysseus
of the possibility that 'she may rob you of your courage and your
manhood' once she had got him into bed. The most traditional of all

heroes, faced with such a patent threat of castration as it is embodied in the horrific spectacle of female appetite, attacks the woman to vindicate and affirm his masculinity and punish her for her lack of chastity, reassigning her to her place. The consequences of this affirmation, mediated in the guaranteed power of the phallus and its co-present fear of castration, re-emerge in 'Canto 47' as Pound's sheer disdain for the female. Although a partner in the sexual act, she has no access to the knowledge and rationality that coitus is supposed to enlighten men with:

Two span, two span to a woman,
Beyond that she believes not. Nothing is of any importance.
. . .
The stars are not in her counting,
        To her they are but wandering holes. (237)

The protection of the power of the phallus is analogous to the defence of monosemy against polysemy: that is, against the productive capabilities that the female seems to epitomise for Pound and which are intrinsically inimical to the fixity of rationality. Indeed, in the passage just quoted, concerning the 'wandering holes', apart from reading a brutal insult to feminity, one might wish to assert that, out of Pound's control, the language points to the female perspective on the universe as being patently deeper, literally more profound than the fixity of masculine rationality and 'counting'. This is just the sort of reading that Pound and his critics cannot consider. In their process of unlocking the mysterium as faithful adherents to the Poundian religion, they defend its suppression of multivalency as in language as in culture.

Few Poundians would be so bold as to declare with D.S. Carne-Ross that 'Pound's whole effort is *not* to be polysemous',[34] even though their whole critical enterprise resides in helping Pound 'to give back to the literal first level its full significance' or, as Donald Davie has it, to revive 'the dead metaphor in the cliché "crystal clear" '.[35] It is in the critics' collective unwillingness to properly avow this about their relation to Pound that Pound's poetry retains its mysterious 'modernity'. It would be tempting to believe Schneidau's prognosis in identifying 'Jakobson's metonymic pole with true creativity in modern literature'[36] but in fact, in Pound's case, metonymy is essentially no more than flirted with as it signals desire. Pound finally reverts to the metaphoric mode, which Jakobson identifies as the trope *traditionally* associated with poetry.

The extent to which desire is allowed to play its part in the *Cantos* depends upon Pound's timing of the intervention of the phallus — 'timing the thunder' (613) as it were. It would appear that desire is allowed its existence only under the firm constraints of the law. The imposition of the law upon desire, upon the metonymic flow, can be readily translated into thematic terms. Throughout the *Cantos* sexuality is prominent but only under the shadow and constraint of duty and propriety. Oddysseus' interlude with Circe's voluptuousness is justified only as part of the ritual he must undertake in his journey towards knowledge. Elsewhere Pound fulminates against usury because it 'lyeth/ between the young bride and her bridegroom' (230), thus threatening the ideal social order by its interruption of sanctified sexuality. It is especially noteworthy that prostitution and concubinage are condemned throughout the *Cantos*, their unproductive nature being considered as flaunting a disregard of natural generation. The propriety of the sexual act, then, depends upon its function. If it is part of the process of natural productiveness then sexuality is celebrated; if not, then it is despised and condemned as perverted.

If it seems that my emphasis on Pound's relation to the phallus as the guarantor of masculine power is exaggerated, one of his many quite scurrilous letters (that have not, naturally enough, been collected and published by any of his disciples) can confirm my view. During the preparation of the Three Mountains Press edition of the first sixteen cantos in 1924, Pound discussed with his printer, William Bird, the initials that Henry Strater had executed for the volume. On 10 April 1924, Pound writes to Bird referring to Strater's initial for 'Canto 4' (see Figure III). At the bottom on either side of the page can be seen what Pound disparagingly refers to as a 'love-knot' and a 'curley-cue'. His objection is to the fact that these figures ressemble the penis, but not the phallus. Many of the points I have been trying to make about Pound in this chapter might be confirmed if I simply quote Pound's outburst: apparently the figures in this design represent

NOT A phallus but a penis
an eunuch's penis = a
      thing that never had any
        significance
save that of a piss-tube —
the phallus is not the cock =
it is the COCK ERECT
        = obj. of worship —
Penis did not inspire primitive religions.[37]

Figure III

ᏐᎻᎬ FOᏌᎡᏐᎻ CᎪᏁᏐO

ALACE in smoky light,
Troy but a heap of smouldering boundary stones,
ANAXIFORMINGES! Aurunculeia!
Hear me. Cadmus of Golden Prows!
The silver mirrors catch the bright stones and flare,
Dawn, to our waking, drifts in the green cool light;
Dew-haze blurs, in the grass, pale ankles moving.
Beat, beat, whirr, thud, in the soft turf
               under the apple trees,
Choros nympharum, goat-foot, with the pale foot alternate;
Crescent of blue-shot waters, green-gold in the shallows,
A black cock crows in the sea-foam;

And by the curved, carved foot of the couch,
      claw-foot and lion head, an old man seated,
Speaking in the low drone . . . :
           Ityn!   Itys
Et ter flebiliter, Ityn, Ityn!
And she went toward the window and cast her down,
     "All the while, the while, swallows crying:
Ityn!
     "It is Cabestan's heart in the dish."
     "It is Cabestan's heart in the dish?
     "No other taste shall change this."
And she went toward the window,
                the slim white stone bar
Making a double arch;
Firm even fingers held to the firm pale stone;
Swung for a moment,
            and the wind out of Rhodez
Caught in the full of her sleeve.
         . . . the swallows crying :
          Bi

This outburst precedes by almost twenty years the crescendo of
assertive and violent utterance that the speeches on Radio Rome in
World War II constitute. It has everything to do the sort of sheer
rhetorical abuse that is exhibited in the following, quite typical passage
against the Jews and the English which Pound broadcast on 21 March
1943:

> Don't start a pogrom. Don't start a pogrom. The problem is not inso-
> uble. Don't start a pogrom; the problem, the Chewisch problem, is
> not insoluble. Don't start a pogrom; SELL 'em Australia. Don't go
> out and die in the desert for the sake of high kikery. Don't die for
> Tel Aviv, and Goldsmid and Jerusalem: SELL 'em Australia. Don't
> GIVE 'em a national home. SELL 'em a national home; if they'll
> buy it. Of course at cut-rates; long-term credit. Firesale terms and
> the rest of it, you'll never get the full price of what you sell 'em but
> it would be cheaper on the whole in the end to SELL 'em Australia.
> They aren't likely to go out and conquer a national home. Of course,
> if they want to, you can sell 'em the guns and munitions. I don't
> think it can be done for cash down. I don't think they will rush out
> to form cohorts and batallions, but try it FIRST if you don't believe
> me. When it has failed, sell 'em Australia. and give 'em Cripps for
> High Commissar, and Eden to be their first Prime Minister; and
> Fatty Temple, clothed in an ephod to serve in the synagogue, or to
> be high priest of his new synthetic religion. Cooking in Westminster
> to support international usury to reverse the decrees of the church,
> and deify usury. With Muddleton Murray, and Norman Angell, and
> Montagu Norman and the Montagues that are not real Montagues, and
> Mocatta and Rothschild. (EPS 255)

Here Pound is using his rhetorical force to issue social *directives* on how
to deal with international Jewry. His whole improbable, but only
partially tongue-in-cheek solution to the problem and his nationalistic
prognoses (compounded with his penchant for assigning a part in the
Jewish conspiracy to non-Jews like Archbishop Temple and Middleton
Murray) are all couched in the *imperative*. But the imperative is ingrati-
ating by force of its adoption of the vernacular, the slang and popular
usages of a shrewdly simple demotic rhetoric. The content and language of the speech typify Pound's faith that the nature of and remedy
for social problems can be conveyed to the people by the force of the
rhetorical edict: this is the discourse of the dictator, installing and
flattering prejudice and misreason in the people.

This is perhaps not the most vituperative or offensive of Pound's speeches against the Jews or the English, but in exhibiting various tropes that are familiar from Pound's discourse over many years it shares the sheerly rhetorical power that enables the editor of the radio speeches to see them as 'The Poor Man's Cantos' (EPS 437). In that judgement, based on the conviction that they are the 'demotic expression of what Pound has been saying for years' (EPS 437) L.W. Doob penetrates quite deeply into the layers of vindication and dissimulation that many other critics have erected around Pound's work. Proceeding from notions as that shared by such critics as Clark Emery, Donald Davie, Leon Surette, namely that the *Cantos* are 'a poetry of emergence' where ideas shimmer on the 'edge of expression', it has been possible for critics to gloss over the obnoxious direction of the rhetoric that Pound unfailingly employs. Often in Poundian criticism that whole tendentious aspect of Pound's work has been subsumed under the blanket heading of anti-Semitism; and this for the very good reason that Pound himself has publicly tried to excuse his failings in that respect. He has been humble and penitent in apologising for 'that stupid, suburban prejudice of anti-Semitism'[38] and has thereby allowed his followers a sort of breathing space (even though it allows other aggressive snobbisms — against suburbanity and decentralisation, for example — to emerge in a way which can be taken to characterise the nature of the drive behind Pound's work generally).

Far, indeed, from being that 'poetry of emergence', the *Cantos* continually aim at the unequivocal expression of Pound's opinions. He himself admits as much: 'No one can accuse me of not trying to communicate what I knew,what I have known, during the past 20 years, often with tactless insistency . . . ' (ESP 172). Some markers on the route of that tactless insistency must be the celebrated Hell cantos, 14 and 15, or the even better known Usura canto, 45; these each are involved in the forthright telling of 'what I have known'. The opening lines of another, 'Canto 52', demonstrate Pound's confidence in his own ability to hand on the truth to the reader:

> And I have told you how things were under Duke
> > Leopold in Siena
> And of the true basis of credit . . . (257)

And this sort of confidence is sustained. The first stages of Pound's personal tragedy occur when the gods in the shape of the American liberation forces in Italy had punished him for his hubristic bent by imprisoning him in the DTC camp at Pisa. There he is supposed to have learnt the humility that is often taken to pervade the Pisan cantos. Yet even in those cantos, where the aridity and arrogance of some of the earlier work are apparently replaced by the repentant lyrical voice, there emerges a clear indication of Pound's refusal to do anything but trust completely and rely upon the correctness of his perception. The famous lyrical passage at the end of 'Canto 81', the 'Pull down thy vanity' section (520-522), is given to the reader as the utterance of an enlightened oracle, as the *lesson* that has been rescued from historical process by careful and privileged contemplation, so that it is now available for transmission as truth. In 'Canto 81' Pound refers to the appearance of the tangible goodness and enlightenment he seeks in the form of seventeenth-century English music — especially that of Henry Lawes and John Jenkyns. That music, the leaf that rises from the root of Waller and Dowland, is capable of establishing a proper tradition, but Pound sees after it 'for 180 years almost nothing'. In fact the revival of interest in that enlightenment was only finally brought about by himself and Arnold Dolmetsch. This perception of his, or his realisation of that beauty, comes with the by now familiar appearance of a 'new subtlety of eyes into my tent', a version of the great epiphany of clarity. This epiphanic moment, not the 'full Εἰδὼς', but what Michael Schuldiner calls the possibility of 'affective knowledge',[39] gives way to the bland statement of its lesson, its import. The 'what thou lovest well remains, the rest is dross' section of this canto conveys nothing other than Pound's knowledge and his confidence in that knowledge. It can be related to the opening of 'Canto 52' which I have just quoted: it embodies the knowledge that man's errors and vanities result from his inability properly to 'Learn of the green world what can be thy place'.

Here, then, the Εἰδὼς has actually made its way into the poem and Pound even congratulates himself on the actual enactment of that knowledge in the prosecution of his poem; he reminds us that 'to have done instead of not doing / this is not vanity'. The claims of the final few lines of the canto seem to cast an ironic light on the assumptions of the whole passage and on the critical attentions it has received: as well as encouraging us to 'Pull down [our] vanity', our emptiness, the passage contains its own vanities, those of self-congratulation. The voice which rhetorically attacks man as a 'beaten dog beneath the hail', as 'Rathe to destroy, niggard in charity' and full of 'mean . . . hates /fostered in falsity' makes an almost comical and certainly brazen, self-righteous epilogue to its attack:

> To have gathered from the air a live tradition
> or from a fine old eye the unconquered flame
> This is not vanity. (522)

Such a paradoxical movement in the text's direction presents another sort of fissure in Pound's rhetorical confidence: as I have already shown, he regards truth to be the ineluctable component of the correct and proper handling of the language. Language for him has the innate ability to close up the gap between its signifier and its signified and so refer directly to the referent. That attitude is plainly enough expressed in a footnote to the essay on Cavalcanti, written as far back as 1910. Referring to the thirteenth-century use of the word 'rhetoric', he says that it 'must not here be understood in the current sense of our own day. "Exact and adequate speech" might be a closer rendering.'[40] The cratic confidence that I have pointed out before in relation to this theoretically rigorous use of language is surely not missing from this canto either: 'the unconquered flame' that emblemises the establishment of 'a live tradition' from historical process contains all the necessary phallic qualities to allow it to stand as the champion of 'thy true heritage' — the richness of natural generation.

Pound's conviction that language is an unremitting part of the natural generative cycle, and that it is uniquely capable of disclosing truth and establishing value is integral to his teleological propaganda. Some support for it he obviously derives from the work he did on the notebooks of Ernest Fenollosa. Fenollosa's most important text, *The Chinese Written Character as a Medium for Poetry*, indulges in the same confusion of metaphor and metonymy as besets Pound. For example, Fenollosa believes that 'relations are more real and more important than the things which they relate.'[41] But by a similar epistemological and metaphorical leap as Pound makes, Fenollosa draws the analogy between that desired state of relatedness and the 'actual and entangled lines of force as they pulse through things'[42] in the natural world. This is in a sense the fundamental Poundian metaphor which assumes that language is co-extensive, analogous and co-operative with the natural world. This, as I have said before, is thereby reductive of language and/ or the natural world to a tautology: the signifier is limited, chained not to another signifier but to the functional expression of the natural world. In other words, it is for the signified that language works in Poundian writing. That signified, given as a sort of knowledge as in 'Canto 81', is the result of a confident and mystical jump from, as Fenollosa betrays it, 'the minor truth of the seen to the major truth of the unseen'.[43] Precisely that 'unseen' is what Pound will reveal, the great ball of crystal that it is his sacerdotal mission to pass on to us:

I have brought the great ball of crystal;
    who can lift it? (795)

Thus the truth for Pound is a given object, a meaning which inheres in the language, as the form of the carving inheres in the stone: it is something to be handed on from writer to reader once the writer has uncovered it. That sort of meaning can be seen precisely as a commodity and one which is not available to the reader for alteration. Pound's priestly supervision of the meaning of his text does, however, often slip: perhaps this is because, like Fenollosa, Pound has glimpsed the relational and reticular structure of language, its metonymic axis, but instead of attaching to that internal perspective he has subsumed it beneath the thrall of a certain overview, a particular ichnographic plan. His ichnographic stance is, of course, the traditional privilege of the transcendent ego. The discoveries of Lacan, via Freud, of the relations of the individual subject to the network of the symbolic, and metonymy's role in the signification of desire, show that privilege to be based on an illusory plenitude — that of the subject who speaks and knows (what he is saying). No more determined an example of such a subject could be found than the tactless and insistent Ezra, the priest.

It is precisely this full 'I' that is the subject of the Cartesian *cogito*. Pound's attention to it seems, at a crude level, to go hand in hand with his fondness of the French language and its culture. Indeed, William Fleming goes so far as to identify that preference exactly with its roots in the Cartesian formula.[44] To this might be added Pound's sympathy with the legendary and mystical clarity that is supposed to inhere in the French language. Furthermore, it is tempting to say that the cultural hegemony that France has tended to exert over the English-speaking world would also have attracted the insistent Pound's admiration. He recognises that draw when he remarks that the English poetic tradition has always looked across the Channel for refreshment.[45] It is clear, in any case, to see that the qualities of clarity and control that are native to the *cogito* and its epistemology are likely to be admirable to Pound, and ones which his whole imperious project can easily and comfortably attach to.

One might guess, then, that although there is a seeming crescendo of egoist confidence in the radio speeches, the whole movement never releases its fundamentally metaphysical grip. Indeed, it would be possible to regard both the radio speeches and the poetry that came after as being dedicated to one and the same end: namely, to the job of rescuing or removing unified subjectivity from the process of language in so far as language threatens that subject's claims to control. I have just shown how the Pisan cantos, for all their enforced humility, propose the knowledge of such a subject. By looking at 'Canto 99' I will show how the later cantos also point to the *utilisation* of such a knowledge and attempt to withdraw its epistemological assumptions from any possibility of attack or interrogation. In the meantime, however, I am intending to propose that the radio speeches mark the summit of many of Pound's aspirations and indicate the fundamentally traditional bases of his thought.

Following on from Pound's assumption that the text can and should convey an already actual but not yet openly perceptible truth, that it can express a pre-existent meaning, we have seen how Pound attempts to lock meaning into his text in such a way as to allow various critics to attempt the unlocking, the transcription of that meaning. Clearly that process enjoins the whole project of *Phaedrus* where the split between expression and meaning, content and form, analogous to the division of body and soul, is reminiscent of Fenollosa's 'minor truth of the seen' and 'major truth of the unseen'. The minor is the letter, the text, while the major is the spirit, the truth. Writing then becomes purely manualistic, conceived of as simply the mnesic trace of whatever truth has been installed there, rather than the truth itself. Writing is necessarily removed from the truth which, in Western metaphysics, is properly expressible only in the authentic voice of the subject: writing is little more than the servant of the voice, of the logos. These conceptions are examined in the work of Jacques Derrida. For him they constitute the 'metaphysics of presence'[46] wherein it is assumed that the truth can reveal itself only by the immediacy of the spoken word, and Saussure's radical realisation of language as a system of material difference is discarded. Derrida's work explicates what sort of distrust for writing has attended Western thinking where the notion of the unified subject allows us — via the subject's voice — to the truth of presence and the present. It is to this phonocentrism, to that faith in the stability of the voice and its concomitant subjectivity, that Pound reverts in his radio broadcasts. The load of the truth and its political position are made totally clear on the short-wave proclamation that this is 'Ezra Pound speakin' from Europe for the American heritage' (EPS 77).

In a very aptly titled radio speech, 'Towards Veracity' (7 March 1943) Pound recalls that it is only 'after two friends determined to break down my antipathy for radio' (EPS 236) that he began to listen to broadcasting. He also recalls this old distrust in a wartime letter to Ronald Duncan.[47] One must assume his dislike to have been formulated on the behalf of a more general attitude to the mechanisation of culture which Pound would see as a process that severed human contact with the natural world. Later, however, his enthusiasm for this direct mode of communication was allowed to emerge from his metaphysical *parti pris* and take a marked role in his poetics. How can we explain the enthusiasm with which he embraced radio except by reference to radio's power to transmit the quality of the subject's voice without the interference of the materiality that stands in the way of writing communication? We have already seen how rigid is Pound's belief in the pure representational ability of language, and here in 'Toward Veracity' we have ample demonstration of his confidence in the possibility of veracity being uttered directly by the voice of the unified subject. As Colin MacCabe puts it, 'Language as representation and truth as presence are two sides of the same coin,'[48] the standard currency employed in the processes of cultural exchange that we have inherited. So Pound's confidence that truth can be announced stems from his belief in representation, and vice versa (as I showed in Chapter 2). His whole attitude becomes the basis for an entire system of values to the point that he feels able to assert that truth alone can be of interest to the individual subject: on the radio 'the interesting talkers were those who were simply telling the truth' (EPS 236). Pound's extremism lies in the ensuing evaluation that he makes which implies that truth and the subject are naturally commensal, neither one properly operable without the other: the 'split man' (GK 343) is incapable of seeing the truth, and the truth, if hidden, causes the perversion of man's morality and institutions. This is simply an extreme humanism.

What Pound and Fenollosa both offer in their theories of poetic language is the elision of the time-lag which characterises writing − or, more specifically, which characterises alphabetical writing. The gap between signifier and signified, between, that is, the acoustic image and the mental concept, is made intolerably large in Pound's eyes by alphabetical writing since alphabetical writing interposes the material letter between signifier and signified. For both these writers in their aspirations towards a language which escapes mediacy the ideogram can become the auspicious emblem of direct and speedy communication since it is supposedly linked in a naturally representational way to the notion it expresses. When Pound mentions that Gaudier-Brzeska, with no formal training in Chinese, was able to read ideograms simply by recognising what they are picturing, he is not only praising Gaudier's intuitive artistic insight but also the ideogram's naturalness.

The ideogram, then, is drawn into the Pound/Fenollosa metaphysical current by being put up as the literal counterpart to a natural process of representation: ' . . . all truth is the transference of power. The type of the sentence in nature is the flash of lightning.'[49] The ideogram is the model for Pound's writing process because it transfers truth in a flash from the origin of truth in the subject. As Herbert Schneidau has put it, this is the ideal of 'nothing less than a way across the terrifying Cartesian gap between internal and external, between subjective and objective'.[50] It is a way of guaranteeing the unity of the subject who speaks as both origin and receiver of truth while doing away with the bothersome materiality of letters.

One of the few Poundian critics to note that Pound's obsession with correct and direct communication is a product of his confidence in the spoken word, a confidence in language being able to cross out the materiality of its own substance, is Max Nänny. Nänny does not, however, make use of his intuition in quite the way that one might expect; rather, in talking about Pound's oral base, he contents himself with describing Pound as a sort of shaman, an 'oral singer . . . a singer of the tribe'.[51] The link with the characteristic prejudices of Western thought is missing from Nänny's account. This leads him to the expediency of just tacking on to the end of his essay, 'Oral Dimensions in Ezra Pound', the observation that 'there is a streak of intolerance, of the totalitarian' in the *Cantos* as in other oral poetry.[52] It is an understatement to which I hope my arguments will have added some flesh: Pound's extreme desire to elide the materiality of language and thus to ensure the unified power of the subject is intrinsically totalitarian. Indeed, the type of writing that he appeals to and approves of, the ideogrammic system, even has in its historical rationale some sort of totalitarian bias. Ideograms, according to one scholar, sprang from 'l'usage généralisé de la forme écrite à des fins administratives', and, furthermore, had important foundations in the staffs and signs of power in early Chinese civilisation, just as the *fasces* did in Rome.[53]

There is no need to disagree with Nänny's suggestion that Pound was in some sense embarrassed by literal writing: that is part of the thrust of my argument so far. Nowhere is the embarrassment more evident than in Pound's continual apologies for *Guide to Kulchur* within that book itself. *Guide to Kulchur* provides ample evidence of Pound's rigorous attitude to the relation of truth to writing: 'I mean or imply that certain truth exists . . . Truth is not untrue'd by reason of our failing to fix it on paper' (GK 295). The process of fixing it on paper is somewhat threatening to Pound's sense of himself as purveyor of truth, but he appears to think that he has achieved some success in the effort. Very often his success has been gained through letters — his own, or those of Malatesta or Adams. Letters, of course, may be conceived of as a sort of compromise between speech and writing. But generally writing is seen, as in Marshall McLuhan's view which duplicates Pound's, to have 'a fragmentary impact on the human sensorium',[54] since it splits away the message from the voice and betrays the subject's split in existence.

In this context, Pound's opting for the radio in order to convey his thoughts and disseminate his truth is an appropriation of the electric age with all its power of 'instant illumination'.[55] The appeal to the modern form of the 'drum telegraph' (LE 77) that Pound makes may be seen in the terms I have already used — metaphor and metonymy. In opting for the instantaneous expression of relations (which is a para- phrase of Pound's own description of what a good metaphor should be), he shies away from the lure of metonymy which is always conno- tative of the split subject, of the 'schismatic tendency' (GK 343), of desire.

In all his manoeuvres Pound is finally interested in the project of confessing his subjectivity at its secure and unified position at the root of the Cartesian *cogito*. It is partly to testify to the reactionary nature of that stance in regard to modernist writing that I am stressing Pound's final return to the metaphoric with all that that implies about the subject's control of desire and language. It seems to me that Pound is finally unable to cope with the very idea of language's productivity, even though he is caught in its usage. His extremist drive towards the direct transmission, with nothing lost, of metaphysical truth from his subjective position founders irrevocably (and quite properly) upon the alphabetical system. It is that system itself which subverts and embarr- asses Pound's poetics. Pound's simple and wilful directive that

> the mould must hold what is poured into it
>   in
>   discourse
>   what matters is
> to get it across e poi basta (486)

could actually never be enough.

4 THE SACRED AMERICAN EDICT

'The plan is in nature rooted' (709), says Pound, deriving this expression for proper social organisation from K'ang-Hsi's *Sacred Edict*, of which 'Canto 99' is largely a version. But that metaphor itself is certainly more deeply rooted than Pound's picking up of F.W. Baller's translation of the Chinese text. It acts as an emblem of the most profound nostalgia which permeates Pound's work and which may be posited as a nostalgia for the institutions and ground of the locus of his first contact with the world, namely the Western frontier town of Hailey in Idaho. Pound's family, on his father's side at least, claimed the status of genuine pioneers. Indeed, Pound was led to believe that his father 'was probably the first white male child born in the northern part of Wisconsin' (PD 16), the state where his grandfather, Thaddeus Coleman Pound, had served as a lieutenant and governor. It is notably to some of the particulars of the political and social formations of the last years of the nineteenth century, so dear to his paternal family, that Pound attaches many of his ideas throughout his entire writing career. His childhood, in other words, provides much of the 'literary capital' (PD 7) that his writing deploys.

Pound feels that 'one could write the whole social history of the United States from one's family annals' (PD 6), and it is precisely his use of that connection that I intend to examine here. In acting out the very linear filial transmission of vital notions and values which he uses as the intrinsic generating metaphor in 'Canto 99', Pound is duplicating many of the notions about American social formation which were prevalent at the end of the nineteenth century – notions which we can assume his family had been somewhat involved in formulating. The light of his father and grandfather's beliefs is the light which bathes the whole process of establishing a given social order and it can be identified very closely with the currents of agrarian and populist thought. The historian Richard Hofstadter has characterised populism by a set of traits that are quite familiar to any reader of the *Cantos*. He talks of the nostalgia for a golden age; a belief in the efficacy of natural harmonies and cycles; what he calls a 'dualistic version of social struggle', a sort of us-and-them mentality; a conspiracy theory of history, akin to Pound's theory of usurocracy; the primacy of money, the importance of which for Pound I am about to show; and, not least, an anti-Semitism to

66

which Pound is an all too obvious heir.[1]

It is probably Pound's sustained and insistent belief in the useful-
ness of the ideas of Thomas Jefferson that indicates best his position as
upholder of a lengthy tradition of agrarian thinking. The Jeffersonian
ideal of a republic constituted by small freehold farmers enjoying self-
sufficiency and social equality is also at the very root of agrarian thinking. It is simply a reaction to the erosion of that ideal in the 1890s that
in fact forms the base of populism. The figure of the self-providing,
assiduous and dignified yeoman appears early in the history of American westward expansion and is clung to hard until the twentieth century, when the prevalence of industrial influence pointed up some of its
painful anachronisms and illusions. That image of the yeoman has been
heavily romanticised and poeticised. Not the least corollary of that
poeticisation is what Henry Nash Smith epitomises as the image of the
'Garden of the World', a

> poetic idea . . . that defined the promise of American life. The
> master symbol of the garden embraced a cluster of metaphors
> expressing fecundity, growth, increases, and blissful labour in the
> earth, all centering around the heroic figure of the idealized frontier
> farmer armed with that supreme agrarian weapon, the sacred plow.[2]

These metaphors of natural process are Pound's too. Hearing him
talk of 'the teething promise' of his nation is to hear him attach to the
agrarian myth. Or when he says that 'I thoroughly believe in plowin' '
(Letters 343), he corroborates the almost mythical status that the
implement assumes in agrarian folklore.[3] Indeed, the primitivistic elevation of the plough to the stars, the Pleiades in 'Canto 47', underlines
the nature of Pound's vision.

In the agrarian mythology the role of the plough is to furnish the
small farmer with not only his subsistence but also with a certain degree
of social dignity. The extent to which the farmer's image was itself
cultivated in American ideology, above and beyond the actual material
conditions of his life, has been dealt with elsewhere.[4] Pound enjoins
that whole ideological tradition whereby the 'simplicity . . . and
naiveté' (695) of those who have contact with the earth helps to constitute their 'moral uprightness' (697). This misleading connection was
necessary for the development in the nineteenth century of the American economy, since it was part of the ideology which enthralled food-
producers and helped to ensure that agriculture developed into a large
enough commercial enterprise to be capable of supplying the needs of

the whole continent: 'Food is the root. Feed the people' (695).

If the general nature of the root can be established for Pound in agrarian culture, the means of distribution also finds a quite deliberate analogy in the history of the American West. For Pound it appears imperative 'and the business of the government to see that *both* production and distribution are achieved' (J/M 69) and the great hope for improved communications at that time was, as predicted and advocated by Jefferson himself, the waterway system and the invention of the steamboat by Fulton: 'Steam-power hastened the transition from subsistence to commercial agriculture.'[5] Thus Pound is enabled to eulogise Jefferson for his perspicacity and his formative role in the American ideology. 'He canalized thought by means of his verbal manifestations' (J/M 15).

In helping to channel the energy and thought of the people who came after him, Jefferson was attempting to put back life into the old metaphor of 'putting things straight,' ensuring that the nation was

> Woven in order,
>> as on cords in the loom (695)

and incidentally undoing the 'knots' (696) that cause disruption and ruin in the modes of production and communication. Many of the central tenets of Pound's system of thought are thus embedded in Jeffersonian action, and they re-emerge in 'Canto 99' and its explicit laying out of the *Sacred Edict*'s directives. The straight lines of Jefferson's thought are indicative of both directness and moral rectitude in all forms of communication − commercial, familial, historical, political, scriptoral and so on. As we saw in the previous chapter, both directness and rectitude are presided over by the masculine principle:

> Man's phallic heart is from heaven
>> a clear spring of rightness (697),

with the notion of 'its aim' (702) adding further connotations of directness. The lines of communication that Pound weaves into his text are self-justifying. The tropes that unite the 'filiality' of father and son to the historical processes of generation between root and leaf and to the lines of the plough and so on all demonstrate Pound's contention that in working on 'our job to build light' we necessarily employ lines of force that are 'non disunia' (694). The function of the waterways was seen in mid-nineteenth-century eyes as that of unifying the nation and thereby revindicating the old revolutionary slogan, '*E pluribus unum.*'

The prospect, then, of 'Canto 99' is social process directed from the root, where the folk have 'solid principles' (696), along coherent lines that effectively 'bind thru the earth', bathed in the unifying light of phallic action. The principle that all the elements of proper communication should 'converge at the root' (694), should 'trace out and bind together' (695), should be 'non disunia', lends itself to the ideogram's structure with its authoritarian aetiology. The tight unity that is supposed to inhere in the etymology of the *ch'eng* ideogram, a man standing by his word in *sinceritas*, is an example of this. Such a principle leads, as J.J. Wilhelm in a rare moment of insight has pointed out, to Pound's idiosyncratic mystical faith (learned from the land and emblemised in the figure of the plough), to his own re-ligio, or tying back together.[6] This is a tying together that reaches its compelling summary in Pound's adoption of Fascism with its own etymological roots in the *fasces*, the staffs of power bound together around the aggressive edge of the axe. The *fasces* in this light can be seen as an alternative but equivalent image to that of the magnet surrounded by fixed lines of force (Figure I).

'Canto 99', then, presents the generating lines of force in language which constitute Pound's attachment to Fascism. In other words, the very language Pound uses is in the thrall of Fascist ideology. Further, it is a language which invests heavily in the notion that the individual can control the natural means of production. As such it is a confirmation of Wilhelm Reich's early analysis of Fascist ideology:

> The basic elements of fascist ideology . . . have an individualistic character. What is collective in fascism stems from the socialistic tendencies in the mass basis, as the individualistic elements stem from the interests of big business and the fascist leadership.[7]

In the 1890s the socialistic tendencies of the populist movement joined forces with the profoundly individualist drift towards profit and big business. The populist farmer 'entered the twentieth century still affected by his yeoman inheritance but with a growing awareness of the businesslike character of his future'.[8] The intellectual voice of the populist movement came, paradoxically enough (as Fascism, too, is a paradoxical marriage of classes), from the section of American society most likely to be antagonistic to the grass-roots culture of the populists, namely the eastern bourgeoisie. Hofstadter explains the lending of their voice to the popular cause as a function of the fact that both classes had been missed out by the rapid and extensive growth of industrial urbanism in the Midwest.[9] It is, similarly, this whole area of the Midwest that Pound's early childhood in Idaho and his subsequent removal to Pennsylvania managed to spare him from: he too, in a sense, missed out that great expanse of industrialism.

The type of the chauvinistic intellectuals who supported the populists might be found in the figure of Emerson with his squire-like presence in Concord; or in Jefferson himself and his ambiguous relationship to those whose labour he exploited. But, added to that almost traditional stance of intellectual apartheid, these supporters of populism exhibit a simple disdain and scorn for the masses – a scorn not hard to see paralleled in the sort of supercilious attitude that Pound praises in Mussolini, who carefully altered his speeches from town to town according to the class of the population he happened to be addressing (J/M 65), or in Jefferson who quite undemocratically 'governed with a limited suffrage and by means of conversation with his more intelligent friends' (J/M 15). When Pound, too, in an unusual pun, dubs the many, the masses, as the 'menée', it is to affirm the necessity of their role in the sage tutelage of the intellectuals:

> meng, the people, the many, the menée,
> > the perishing.
> Sage men have plans. (695)

At least part of the reason that Pound thought the results of the Homestead Act were to be so much abhorred was the 'greed and imbecility' (J/M 121) of the people to whom land was given: their energy was unbridled by the better judgement of an intellectual plan.

Thus a split in the ideological fabric between the intellectual and the agricultural worker appears, and it is one which continually embarrasses Pound. His inability to reconcile the two is nowhere more obvious than in the weave of 'Canto 99' itself, an extremely dense and difficult political tract hoping to 'Illumine the words of procedure' (698), to 'talk modus' (704) and establish a 'Precise terminology [as] the first implement' (711). The controls attributed to intellectual power over the dignified labour of the masses can be rewritten as a certain predominance given to culture over nature, or to man's elaboration of his natural root. In attaching to the particulars of the agrarian mythology, and corroborating what I have said before about 'Canto 47', Pound would see the land as a mother-land, ready to be silent and elided inspiration for male work and creativity. If it is true to say that Pound's roots are steeped in the soil of native American Transcendentalism, then here is an example. Hofstadter has pointed out how in the armatures of the American agrarian mythology the earth is seen as 'characteristically a mother, trade a harlot, and desertion from ancestral ways a betrayal that invited Providential punishment',[10] Pound's fulminations against both harlotry and organised large-scale commerce (that is, commerce organised outside of the simple system of exchange that is epitomised by the Jeffersonian ideal of 'a thousand peasants each growing his own food in his own fields' (J/M 45)) can be thus viewed as a sort of anxiety about contact with the mother-land.

Above, I spoke about the plough and its role in the ideology of mid-nineteenth-century America. The plough in 'Canto 47' becomes an instrument of masculine, phallic power as it aggressively cuts into the passive earth to inseminate it and bring about, in Benjamin Franklin's words, the 'real increase of the seed thrown into the ground, a kind of continuous miracle wrought by the hand of God in [man's] favour'[11] and to confirm, in Emerson's terms, that in nature we can witness 'the endless circulations of the divine charity nourishing man'.[12] The implement permits man to take advantage of the mystical and poetic ability of the earth to flatter, by her productivity, man's rational ordering. The plough, as implement, works as it does in 'Canto 99' first to produce food and second to endow 'simplicity' on those who by its agency forge an unproblematic relationship with the maternal earth. The return to the abundant, food-producing earth is the return of the human being to the mother's breast and thus to an easeful simplicity of the pre-Oedipal stage, where demand and need have not yet been dilacerated and the question of the gap, the lack produced by fear of separation, has not been broached. It is to this desire for a return to such a reliable position that so many of the characteristics of Pound's thought and writing can be referred.

In particular, Pound's obsession with the simplicity (or, in Freud's celebrated expression, the 'oceanic' feeling) of the pre-Oedipal stage has its analogy in the workings of Fascist ideology. The pre-Oedipal stage is the locus for the ease that 'exclusive attachment to the mother'[13] can offer. A return there is like the apparent offer of Fascism to free its subjects from troublesome ideological struggles and to reinstate them in a sort of social simplicity and innocence. The trenchantly individualistic thrust of such a removal can be seen in the ensuing apparition of a concept of history as the expression of the will to power (or to order) in the individual protagonist. It is a view of history that would be at home in the mouth of Carlyle: as William Chace explains it, it is an expression of politics as 'a kind of hero-worship'.[14] There could be no more unequivocal way of looking at Pound's assembling of a body of heroes in a list of proper names, from Malatesta and Odysseus, through Confucius and Jefferson to Mussolini and Major Douglas.

These proper names can be viewed as displacements of the name-of- the-father, of Homer Pound. Fascist ideology, as Reich points out, not only implies the sort of 'idolization of motherhood' that I have been suggesting, but also expresses the 'childish need for protection . . . disguised as the form of feeling at one with the führer'[15] or the father who has taken the mother(land) as his bride (as Deutschland is the bride of the Führer of National Socialism). The repressed conflict that occurs for Pound with his father's name has obvious (£-ian) economic overtones which I will deal with: for the moment, however, it is important to see how Pound's Fascistic thinking is pre-figured in his infantile relations. The anti-psychoanalytical bent of one of his biographers, Michael Reck, suggests that the fact that Pound 'idolized his parents' is sufficient to remove him to safety from the threat of Freudian speculators; but this approach seems unable to recognise the importance of understanding Pound from the point of view of work done on Fascism itself, and it certainly ignores the extent to which the Fascistic 'feeling at one' invests the very roots of Pound's thought.[16]

Pound's regression to the motherland of Idaho and its cultivation by the plough is none the less unstable. He himself insists that 'I did not grow up in Hailey' and refuses to view his first eighteen months as of any importance.[17] But this refusal is in itself an indication of the need to defend against the recognition of parental relations as they are capable of producing disturbance, and the ambivalence of the Oedipal relations. Pound's father is described as 'the naivest man who ever had good sense' and his mother as 'the most discerning person in a rather limited environment'.[18] The qualifications and ambivalance that have settled into these statements can be related to the realisation of the action of the father, the plough, upon the mother, the land: precisely, the primal scene. The much admired elegiac tone of the following lines from 'Canto 47' can be read as at once denying any such realisation of the mother's carnality and yet at the same time affirming the phallic activity of the father (if we remember that 'Weight' is Pound's metonymic formulation of his family name in 'Indiscretions'[19]). Here is a perfect ambivalence:

So light is thy weight on Tellus

Thy notch no deeper indented
Thy weight less than the shadow
Yet hast thou gnawed through the mountain
        Scilla's white teeth less sharp. (238)

The passage through the mountain assumes the connotation of the frontiersman forging through the obstacles of the land, making for a new settlement: Pound's grandfather, of course, was just such an active and integral proponent in the joint railroad and waterway projects to 'make us one country in heart as in government'.[20]

In a manner which 'Canto 99' illustrates, the phallic activity of the plough, the weight, on the land is a vital constituent of the ideal Fascist state. By a process of metonymy Pound links the implemental nature of the plough with the single human body — and incidentally illustrates yet again his and Fascism's claim to have 'respect for the human being as an individual' (PD 11):

People have bodies
        ergo they sow and reap
Soldiers also have bodies,
        take care of the body as implement
It is useful
To shield you from floods and rascality. (705/6)

The *Sacred Edict* establishes the body as a zone of defence, a function that emerges quite signally immediately after the idea of bodies sowing and reaping (which, of course, I am reading here as sexual activity). The body then is seen as the human root to all process and in its reproductive capacity (its delicacy that has to be defended against promiscuity and corruption, 'floods and rascality', or from the *excess* and *absence of rectitude* that Pound so fears) it acts as the paradigm for the ideal state: 'The State is corporate/as with pulse in its body' (737). Indeed, in line with Pound's notion that 'one could write the whole social history of the United States from one's family annals' is his contention, established in 'Canto 99', that 'the whole tribe is from one man's body ' (708).

This linking of the state and the individual body constitutes nothing less than the etymological (in the word 'corporate') and teleological justification of the Fascist male's 'complete identification with the state power'.[21] It is a ploy that operates within an ideological context where language guarantees the structures and causalities of the natural world and thereby attracts to itself corroboration of Pound's claim that it itself is 'natural'. In positing and offering some sort of proof for a set of causal equations, Pound is able to justify the whole network of linguistic connections that structures 'Canto 99'.

It is interesting to see that this particular canto abounds with etymological and phonological puns by which the vital connections are made. Puns such as 'the many, the menée', the 'filiality' of the lines of heritage, the phallic 'uprightness' of moral correctness, the fact that the 'State is corporate' and so on, all centre around an originating pun on the word 'generation': the text of the canto is generated from a concern with the generative capacities of nature and man's ability to hand on 'a live tradition' from generation to generation along the straight lines of moral certitude which are finally analogous to (or mimetic of) the direct *rays* of light from the primogenitary source of the universe, the *sun*, provider of all illumination and clarity. The canto is thus a fascinatingly complex (and untypically cohesive) example of Pound's writing method since it constitutes a network of relations that actually generate the *body* of Pound's thinking. It is itself the very 'convergence' (709) of linguistic tropes that could constitute the illumination that Pound seeks to bring to the world in his role as crusading son. Pound's complaints in later life about the failed coherence of his thought and writing can to some extent be mitigated by the craft of 'Canto 99'.

But, for all that, it is feasible to regard 'Canto 99' as simultaneously the locus of all Pound's confusions. Here, at the very moment of the attainment in writing of his 'plan', the model for the Fascistic *idea statale*, with its workings guaranteed by the appositely named document of the *Sacred Edict*, we find a complex system of linguistic felicities (what Francis Ponge is in the habit of calling *trouvailles*) set out in metonymic glory only to be finally subsumed by the presence of the phallus in the metaphor, demonstrably biographical as well as literary, which tells us that the root is in natural process. At one level it is tempting to be seduced by 'the filiality that binds things together' (686) in this text; at another it is impossible not to recognise the manipulations and machinations of a subject who is supposed to know, the subject who establishes himself as the assuming and confident origin of utterance that is verifiable. And it is the thrust of all that I have been saying that usually this subject both does not know and ignores the *weight* of what he is saying: and so at moments when, as in this canto, the irrational tropes of language, embodied in the pun and metonymic transmutations, are exploited the question must arise as to why they are usually disregarded. The answer seems to indicate that the subject's temporary incursion into those tropes is tendentious and renders uncomfortably gratuitous all other moments of refusal of that productiveness.

Pound's place as subject is largely formulated, then, by his relation to the mother-land. But it is a relationship which is anything but simple. Obviously the influence of the paternal side of the family is very strongly there too, as root. Michael Reck's biography points out that the career of Pound's grandfather, in Congress and with the Union Lumbering Company (where he issued his own money for wages in the form of scrip and in a gesture of autocratically stamped authority), 'must have influenced Pound's own attitudes'.[22] David Heymann goes so far as to say that the allegiance that Pound owes to his grandfather's ideas (a mixture of agrarian and labour sympathies on a base of his paternalistic attitude to business) indicates that 'in this sense Ezra Pound had never abandoned the frontier'.[23] It is to that time, then, precisely in an interstice of nature and culture where it would be possible to idealise and idolise, that Pound's regressive tendencies converge; it is there, between the weighty demands of the name-of-the-father and the earthy comfort of the mother (Tellus), between Laius and Jocasta, that 'the infant Gargantua' (PD 39) assumes his own unified weight, conflating into an apparently unthreatening metaphor the parental forces which normally collude to open up the gap which the subject sutures by means of his assumed subjectivity. It is when that gap is reaffirmed in Pound's experience of the world and language that the illusory plenitude of that subjectivity is called upon to refortify itself. Metaphorically that gap can be reconstituted as the Pound family's eastward journey across the United States when Pound was eighteen months old.

The distance from the petit-bourgeois life in Pennsylvania and the individualistic adventures of the Western ethos elides all those areas of production that sprang up in the mid-nineteenth century in the middle parts of America. All that profitable expansion constituted a virtual disappearance of the old agricultural ideals; accordingly, Pound's traversal of that space, removing or ignoring its troublesome productive capacity, is equivalent to an ignorance about the nature of America and her economic formations. Pound's generalised rejection of the industrial and mechanical age can be traced back to this early removal to the east coast from the Western frontier. But the recognition of that gap most importantly recalls 'Canto 12', where Confucius is quoted thus:

'Wang ruled with moderation,
'In his day the State was well-kept,
'And even I can remember
'A day when the historians left blanks in their writings
'I mean for the things they didn't know,
'But that time seems to be passing.' (60)

The nostalgia for the well kept state is indicative of a similar nostalgia for the characteristics of Western institutions and life on Pound's part. The regretful tone in which Confucius' recognition of historical lacunae is delivered is reminiscent of the whole movement of Pound's *Cantos* and the tensions the poem contains between the shattered incompleteness of experience, the *paradiso spezzato*, and the beatific vision of complete oneness in the unified light of the great crystal. These tensions obviously have to do with Pound's relation to America and his movement across it. Even Pound, for all his repressive tendencies, can remember the existence of the gap and so has to acknowledge it even in traversing it and working against its implications.

It is exactly in its constituting lack that this gap and the crossing of it assume noteworthy importance. In Pound's later snobbism towards the Midwest, especially at the time of his ill-fated appointment as an 'Instructor with professorial functions'[24] at Crawfordsville, Indiana, which ended with his semi-dishonourable dismissal, might be seen the processes of a certain defensiveness against the gap I am speaking of, and thus another articulation of his relation to the lost object which is the instigator of his pervasive nostalgias. Lack is experienced as a function of the subject's submission to the Oedipal schema: to attain full subjectivity the subject is called upon to close over the gap of desire and assert his possession of the phallus under the gaze of paternal law, or his father's possession of the phallus. This affirmation is continually threatened, of course, by the experience of an overlapping series of lacks instituted in a fear of castration and in recognition of the apparent maternal lack.

In an important article, 'La Compromission Poétique',[25] Marcelin Pleynet has seen one articulation of this whole drama within the very name, Ezra Pound. The surname, transmitted by the father, takes on precisely the legal 'Weight' of authority and correct judgement. Homer Pound is characterised in Pound's writings by his ability to assume the role of an incredibly sensitive and accurate judge, a role over-determined by his position as Assayer in the Philadelphia Mint:

I have known Rip to weigh a man's name on his visiting card. Very simple. You weigh the card, then you have the man write his name on it in pencil; then you weigh the card with the signature. This is, however, quite a stunt. (PD 50)

Pound's ambivalence to the father can be seen once again in this passage. The assayer's trick is 'very simple' but none the less admirable in that it is 'quite a stunt'. Of Homer's other feats of judgement as assayer and arbiter of legal fiscal measure, Pound notes that 'Any fool might do it, with infinite patience' (PD 50).

Against his father's possession of the judgemental power of the law the 'infant Gargantua' plots, according to Pleynet, the course of his forename, Ezra. In its identification with the Old Testament priest who weighs out gold and silver we can see not only another aspect of Pound's sacerdotal aspirations but also the element of competition with the father. It is a competition whose movement and terms are manifest in the playing with his own name (the forename, that is). Homer's squinting evaluative assays are emulated by Ezra's all-seeing 'X-Ray'[26] (and I shall show later through H.D.'s terror of Pound what phallic propensities that nominal transformation involves). In another mutation the capitalised RA of Pound's signature is noted by Pleynet as the epitome of phallic utterance: he quotes the phonetician's view that the apical R is 'un son phallique, un représentant de la pulsion génitale'.[27] Furthermore, that RA is pronounced as 'ray', an indication of its connection with the prime source of generative power, the sun.

It is this very drama that is called to mind by Pound's mutilated quotation from Rabelais as it is supposed to relate to his own childhood:

Et celuy temps passa comme les petits enfans du pays c'est assavoir: a boire, manger et dormir . . . Tousjours se vaultroit par les fanges, se mascaroit le nez . . . il se mouschoit à ses manches . . . patronilloit par tout lieu . . . beuvoit en mangeant sa soupe, mangeoit sa fouace sans pan, pissoit contre le soleil, s'asséoit entre deux selles le cul à terre, etc., et gardoit la lune des loups. (PD 41)

In alluding to this chapter of Rabelais, which I have attached in translation to my text in the Appendix, Pound gives us information about his own childhood drama. The 'infant Gargantua' is 'brought up and disciplined in all necessary ways; such being his father's orders'. But against the father's law the infant indulges in a whole range of somatic rebellious effluxes and demonstrations of his anality: rolling in mud, pissing, shitting in his shirt, farting, vomiting, scrawling on paper, sleeping with animals and so on. And at the same time he 'was already beginning to exercise his codpiece', ready to display and assert his fantastic penis (given that status by the great delight the women around him take in it, as much as by his very name) in the context of his father's restrictive law. And, of course, the whole narrative is accompanied by the familiar threat of castration: 'I shall cut it off then.'

This chapter of Rabelais mimes the movement of transgression against the sterling qualities of Homer Pound that can be seen in the inscription of the word *usura* into Pound's name: Ez(u)ra. Usury is the corruption of the very standards Ezra's father is employed to guarantee, check and maintain. 'Usura is a murrain' (229), breeds 'canker' (230) and 'crab-lice', is a 'syphilis' (63), and is thus the very disease which could infect the father with death or diminution of his phallic power. Thus there is at work in the name Ezra Pound an actual and persistent inscription of the struggle against the establishment of his father's phallic law. The attempt of the little Ezra to assert his possession of the phallus is continually beset by the worry that the father already has the phallus and that Ezra may be castrated. Against the perversity of his (ezurocratic) attack on his father, Ezra is led to fetishise the phallus and, as we have already seen in many different manifestations, to revindicate its masculine integrity and wholeness. According once again to Pleynet, the screen memory which is fixed as a sort of defence against the possibility that Rip might weigh up the subject of the name Ezra Pound and see his true value, his true ambivalence, and which at the same time incorporates that ambivalence, is exactly the episode of the visiting card.

In his assumption of the phallus as the instrument whereby masculinity may be vaunted in its gifts of judgement and legality, Pound, as I have said, none the less recognises the condition of castration. His defence against the lacks and separation that his childhood memories lead to is made by way of denying the value of those memories, on the grounds that they do not accord with the retrospective and rationalised intuitions of the full subject of Pound's normative discourse since they come from an underdeveloped phase in 'one's' evolution. It is a sort of tautological rationale:

Only dubious value can attach to a period when one's powers of observation, such as they were, would seem to have exhausted their results in the kinesis of mimicry and to have left but the scantiest subjective record and of which period there seems to be no spoken tradition. (PD 43)

Similarly, in the postscript to 'Indiscretions' where Pound's childhood is inscribed as anything but a scanty impression, Pound offers the reprinting, the repetition of the text, as a way of filling 'a gap' in history (PD 50). The text acknowledges that gap but disclaims it in a contradictory movement: Pound, in fact, wishes that someone 'with more vigour and enthusiasm' (PD 50) could do the job for him.

Such marks of the recognition of lack are all over Pound's textual surface. The establishment of the phallus as a privileged signifier, halting the slide of metonymy and subjecting it to the law of metaphor, has already been noted; but concomitant with that elevation of the phallus is a fierce rejection of anality. That question is continually recurrent in Pound's work and is as often as not linked with the 'gold-bricks' (the pounds of conflated weight and value) in the underground vaults of his father's place of work. The topography of the Philadelphia Mint, as I appeal to it, is made apparent by the presence in the upper rooms of 'an old five-barrelled howitzer' (PD 47) around which Homer and his staff would gather; down below, on the other hand, are the 'bowels of the institution'. In the bowels are the gold and silver whose *expulsion* into the world is *regulated* by the phallic authority exercised by Homer and his instruments – all the 'private possessions of Rip's' (PD 48) that the young Pound notices in the Mint. The infantile memories are here, too, apologised for because of their possible unclarity, but Pound can recall well enough 'avoiding . . . the bowels of the institution' just as he had felt embarrassed by his presence – 'unexplained except by consanguinity' – at a visit to the English Mint later in his life: on that latter occasion too he was relieved 'to not . . . burrow into the vitals of the institution' (PD 45).

The picture that can be adduced to preside over the fear and conse-quent repression of anality appears not, signally enough, in 'Indiscre-tions', but much later in Pound's life during a 1962 interview with Donald Hall. Describing there a re-counting of US coin in the under-ground light of the Mint Pound says:

All the bags had rotted in these enormous vaults, and they were heaving it into the counting machines with shovels bigger than coal shovels. The spectacle of coin being shovelled around like it was litter – these fellows naked to the waist shovelling it around in the gas flares — things like that strike your imagination.[28]

The passage suggests a certain displeasure at the treatment of money as if it were of no value and shovelled around as if it were refuse, the residuum of a process of rotting in the bowels. Pound's revulsion against such an image is repeated in a letter to Felix Schelling in 1922: 'certain things [are] excrement, they will stay in [the] human colon and poison it' (Letters 181).

There is perhaps too an element of homosexual fantasy (also to be repressed) in the figures of these half-naked men, marking the link between anality and sodomy. We know that, to Pound. sodomy is the most unproductive of all expressions of sexuality. Pound's fascination with this scene can thus be illuminated by Freud's rubric for the particular sublimation of anal eroticism as in some way unhygienic: 'Dirt is matter in the wrong place,'[29] The 'wrong place', the bowels that should be avoided, is the locus of dirt and rotten matter. That matter has been metonymised in Pound's writing, as Freud has already noted in his patients, into gold and silver: 'money is the excrement of hell'[30] and 'the anus is a gold-mine.'[31]

The relation of anality to Pound's language can be seen to be an anxious and repulsed one. All reference to anality in the *Cantos* link it with perversion and transgression of the law, and thus with the general corruption of standards and values. The notable carrying agent, the disease, by which such degradation is effected is, of course, *usura* with its disregard for the natural processes of increases: anality is, in Pound's book, similarly unnatural since it will not conform to the phallic law. The usurers are at once sodomites and

the perverts, who have set money-lust
Before the pleasures of the senses. (61)

Pound himself links his memories of his father as he tests the underground matter to his own 'habit of testing verbal manifestations'.[32] If he had not pointed out (by this and references to the usurers as 'perverters of language' (61)) the way to a connection of this anal anxiety and the question of language (a matter in the same circuits of exchange as gold, and a matter which, as I have shown, Pound also tries to repress) then Maud Ellmann might have done it for him. Her article, 'Floating the Pound', utilises the Lacanian notion that

the anal level is the locus of metaphor — one object for another, give the faeces in place of the phallus. This shows you why the anal drive is the domain of oblativity, of the gift. Where one is caught short, where one cannot as a result of the lack give what is to be given, one can always give something else. That is why, in his morality, man is inscribed at the anal level.[33]

In the faeces, the gold offered for the lack of the phallus, the materialist Pound, as he watches the matter in the flickering light of the underground metonymically changing from gold to shit, recognises the ciphers of lack. He attempts to avoid what their significance, their metonymic sliding, subtends by making an oblation of words all subsumed under the primary metaphoric device of the phallus. The 'infant Gargantua' furthermore tells us of his extraordinarily precocious command over words; he is already prodigiously endowed.

The vituperation which attends Pound's dealing with this area of his displeasure, set beneath the panoply of the effects of anality, can be seen as a vindication of Freud's reference to the 'rage and revenge-fulness'[34] that often emerge as a corollary of repressed anal eroticism. Those excessive and vindictive repetitions of charges of genitality in the wrong place are rages against the lack instituted by fear of castration. At the same time as being the register where the word is given in place of the lack, the vituperative force implicitly recognises the existence of lack and thus desire. It is, therefore, in a dialectic of recognition and disavowal that the *Cantos* work themselves out and are articulated. That dialectic is presided over by the erection of the phallus as primary signifier, as the law which governs the unbridled passage of desire across the subject's lack. The repression of anality and the restoration of the upper parts of the Mint's topography are the necessary consequence of this establishment of the phallus. Indeed, when Donald Hall in his interview with Pound broaches the topic of Pound's economic formation in his childhood experience, a certain annoyance consistent with Pound's suspicion of anything that smacks of Freudianism emerges from the response: 'You can go on for a long time on that,' he says,[35] as if to dismiss the question, and then does go on, uttering the material that I have been dealing with.

Some part of the rationale for the subject's refusal of anality in the interests of the controlling phallus is succinctly put by A.E. Durant:[36]

although erotic pleasure in the anal stage of infancy may be controlled by a retention of the sphincters, in general the anus locates a bodily efflux or discourse which is a constantly repeated losing.

> Anality bespeaks submission to those discharges or discourses of the body and is a falling short or lack in the subject which transgresses any assumption of autonomy at the genital level.

Finally, then, it is in the interests of the autonomy and the imaginary completeness of the subject that anality, an uncontrollable loss or separation figuring the possible loss of the phallus, is rejected. The subsequent role of the phallus owes its controlling function to that rejection and so the subject can claim his undividedness and recognise himself in the arrestation of the metonymic drive of desire within the bounds of the law.

What I have been suggesting throughout my work on Pound is that the anxieties which accompany the hoped-for stopping up of the gap in being in Pound's history (which accompany, in other words, the founding of a plenary subjectivity) are linked with Pound's linguistic, economic and political beliefs and ideals (as far as those things can even be separated) in a completely fundamental manner. The concern for 'the testing of verbal manifestations' for their ability to duplicate nature; the rage for the 'true basis of credit' where value could be unequivocal and married to the natural world; and the call for the unified state epitomising order and natural discipline; all these can be seen as compelling symptoms in the struggle to accede to a self-sufficient and masterful (mastering and yet mastered) ego. Wherever the threat of the uncontrollable poses itself — be it in the libido, in language, in economics, or in politics, or even in the 'chaotic' existence of women — the phallocratic edict is pronounced.

To make the sort of attack that I am on Pound's melding of the qualities of the full subject and his idealist notions of language and exchange is effectively to impugn the very 'root' of a certain line of the American heritage. It is a line, played out to some extent by the 1890s, which can be identified (to transmute the statement of Pound's which began this chapter) in 'Nature', or rather in the seminal text of that name by the great progenitor of American culture, Ralph Waldo Emerson. 'Nature' lays out in quasi-philosophical discourse many of the fundamental and constitutive assumptions of Pound's view of man's relation to natural process; in so doing it guarantees Pound in his establishing the ego as a masterful and central *presence* in the world. Many of Emerson's expressions are Poundian (or Fenollosan) in the extreme. According to Emerson, 'man . . . is placed in the centre of beings, and a *ray* of relation passes from every other being to him.'[37] That relation positions man at the heart of the creation, the green world from which he must know his place, a world that is in its disposition 'a discipline of the understanding of intellectual truths'.[38] It is a harmonic and certain model offering 'ministry . . . for the profit of man',[39] 'the endless circulations . . . nourishing man'.

The most apposite slogan for Pound's whole writing practice can be found in 'Nature', where praise is given to the single transcendent figure 'whose eye can integrate all the parts, that is, the poet'.[40] That expectation of Emerson's hovers over the *Cantos*. But Pound's very failure, too, is inscribed in Emerson's writing. The transcendentalist accounts for the sort of incoherence that the twentieth century and a peculiar set of lived circumstances imposed on Pound by the fact that for most ordinary men, even from their supposed central and originary position in nature's theatre,

> the axis of vision is not coincident with the axis of things, and so they appear not transparent but opake. The reason why the world lacks unity and lies broken and in heaps is because man is disunited with himself.[41]

It is exactly against all suggestion and manifestation of the 'schismatic tendency', given after Freud as the subject's fundamental condition, that Pound tirelessly crusades.

But the presumptions of the Emersonian version of the *cogito* had already been systematically threatened by the time of Pound's birth. The dismantling of that literary ethos, described by Larzar Ziff as culminating with 'the defeated of the nineties' and described by Beer in his humorous book *The Mauve Decade*, coincides with the breakdown of the old agrarian mythology. The 'sage of Concord' (134) and his works become the largely unspoken locus of Pound's rigid, but idiosyncratic, version of Descartes' formula. Yet the *cogito* turns in Pound's hands to 'Amo ergo sum.' This is anything but an acceptance of the fact that for the twentieth century, and after Freud, *desidero* replaces *cogito*: rather, it is an expression of the limited recognition of desire as it works against the fortifications of the ego. As I have shown, the limited acceptance of desire on Pound's part is involved with an extreme defensiveness against it.

It may be said, finally, that the installation of the *amo* against the *cogito* is a deceptive strategic ploy: where, after all, are Pound's love poems? The assumption of love in the *Cantos* is nothing other than the experience, profoundly individualistic, of the great crystal, the 'transparent eyeball' that, in Emerson, claims in contradiction to itself that

'I am nothing' but yet 'I see all.'[42] In fact, love is for Pound the entrenched position of the Cartesian subject, infatuated with its own feelings, as it fastens to the object by the visual drive, by the scopic energy which Lacan tells us frees us most easily from the fear of castration and epitomises the subject's most utter control.[43] The providential all-seeing eyeball on the American Seal of 1776 might in this respect act as Pound's motif. The control of the authoritarian subject is symbolised in the eagle of idealism: sight exercises a restraint over language and desire.

PART TWO

' . . . speaking eddies
thru coiled shells:'

Louis Zukofsky 'A, 22'

5 JOYCE: ONE BEDAZZLED EYE

(i) Sight

In his Imagist days, in 1913, Pound defined the ideal poetic image in the following terms:

> An 'Image' is that which presents an intellectual and emotional complex in an instant of time . . . It is the presentation of such a 'complex' instantaneously which gives that sense of sudden liberation; that sense of freedom from time limits and space limits; that sense of sudden growth, which we experience in the presence of the greatest works of art. (LE 4)

As Forrest Read has pointed out, the American Seal struck after the 1776 Revolution fits precisely the criteria for the 'Image'.[1] Pound's insistence on the need for a return to the values of the early days of the American Republic is implicated with his notion of the proper use of language and so with the 'Image' as it presides over the institution of that Republic. In its details, the Seal also corroborates my contentions about the inherently Fascistic and idealist nature of the operations on language which Pound recommends. For my purposes here the Seal (Figure IV) most importantly features, on the one side, the all-seeing and benevolent eye on top of an incomplete pyramid; and on the other side, the profiled eagle that clutches the American states together in a disturbing simulacrum of the *fasces*: all this is in turn presided over by the revolutionary motto, 'E pluribus unum'. The unity that the eagle side of the seal bespeaks is blessed by the unseen god who 'Annuit Coeptis' (favours our beginnings) and by the benevolent eye over the pyramid.

It is that eye which guarantees the revolutionary idealism of 1776. It provides for the institution and constitution of the revolution by what Georges Bataille would call 'une illumination utopique' — the impossible locus, in fact, of Pound's own illuminating crystal. The imperial eagle itself can have similar fantastic claims. In another context Jeffrey Mehlman, bringing together the work of Bataille and Jacques Derrida, points out the idealism explicit in the picture of the imperial eagle, 'un aigle', in Bataille's phrase, 'au-dessus des aigles, un *suraigle* abattant

Figure IV

les impérialismes autoritaires' (which in the case of the American eagle would be the British and their control of American social and economic functions).[2] The eagle is located in this idealist role by a punning reference to Hegel's idealism as it is embedded in the latter's name, thus: 'Son nom est si étrange. De l'aigle il tient la puissance impériale et historique. Ceux qui le prononçent encore à la française [aigle]. . . ne sont ridicules que jusqu'à un certain point.'[3] It is within

the context of the idealist connotations of the Seal's Imagistic iconography, inscribed within the medal's closed and self-sufficient ground
(the garden of the world), that Pound's ideal identification of himself
and his writing operates: the bearer of the Emersonian paradigmatic
eye hopes to function as an imaginary plenitude, Lacan's subject of
certainty; or, in other words, the full subject, caught up in a purely
imaginary specular relation to itself and infatuated with its own feelings.

Mehlman's intervention into the texts of Bataille and Derrida draws
its impulse from a certain laughter, a hilarity which is the reaction to a
certain rotting away − to the impossibility − of the closure of exactly
the Utopian specular relation that can be projected from the Seal's
iconography, and which was prized and asserted continually in Pound's
insistence on the efficacy of the American bourgeois revolution.
Pound's whole political project is an attempt to return to a certain perfection or focus (476) in the realm of clarity, to the setting of the
'sparkling brilliants' which typify, in Marx's prognosis, the spirit of
eighteenth-century revolutions. Pound tries to revivify that spirit in
the face of the 'long depression' that Marx held to result from such
euphoric revolutions.[4] Georges Bataille goes a little further than Marx's
analysis by claiming that the spirit of eagle-eyed idealism 'aboutit
naturellement à l'échec de la révolution' which discovers an ultimate
resting place in the 'satisfaction du besoin éminent d'idéalisme à l'aide
d'un fascisme militaire'[5] − at which point we might see an impossibility of laughter.

But there is a proper locus for Mehlman's hilarity and it is in
Bataille's wonderful notion of the pineal eye. Constituting precisely a
perversion of the pure and clear vision of the idealist, Emersonian eye,
the pineal eye is an organ at the top of the head, looking like a
baboon's anus and releasing all those effluxes and discourses that Pound
has spent so much energy in repressing. Or, perhaps, the locus could be
in the similar anal pulsions of excess and fun which flow out of *Finnegans Wake*, a book which Pound never could abide, and which with its
circular connecting form plays with exactly the specular closure of the
book that Derrida's work has pointed out as the *modus operandi* of
humanist writing. Pound prefers to have a book which is the 'theological encyclopaedia . . . the book of man' vindicated by Hegel's thought:
Pound cannot, on the other hand, comprehend the Joycean project as
it assembles a 'fabric of traces marking the disappearance of an erased
man' and embarks upon an 'adventure, expenditure without re-
serve'.[6]

Pound's investment in the closed specularity of idealism has a devolved symptom in his overt concern with the wholeness of his own imagined image, and concomitantly with the completeness of the body as a homogeneous entity. Pound fears the alteration of the body, as of the image. In one of his letters he tries to sympathise with Wyndham Lewis who has just undergone surgery: trying to imagine which part of the body could best be operated upon without inconvenience he rejects consideration of any – even the buttocks being inviolable (Letters 118). In his use of language that fear of alteration and desire for homogeneity emerge most interestingly in the editing process that he so diligently pursued throughout his life, aiming to 'put one's finger on a slip or a momentary inattention' and thus to clamp down on any sliding away from the intense direction of the lines of light moving from the all-seeing eye: and this in order to 'tighten up the idiom' and so halt the anal flow of excess that is epitomised in *Finnegans Wake* (Letters 251).

At another level the same fear is expressed in a couple of letters Pound wrote to Joyce and in which he discusses the possibility of sending Joyce a photograph of himself.[7] His protective feelings about his own image are clear when he relates his doubts about 'a photo of a portrait of me, painted by an aimiable jew who substituted a good deal of his own face for the gentile parts of my own', and about another 'which represents me as a chinless diplomat from the Balkans'. Another photograph is rejected because (like the childhood information given in 'Indiscretions') it is 'excessively youthful' and thus 'deceptive'. Even the most acceptable of the images, one approved by his father-in-law because it presents 'a sinister but very brilliant italian' and by his landlady as 'it is the only photograph that has ever done you justice', is embarrassing because of its suggestion of 'the good man of Nazareth' and is finally labelled 'seductive and sinister'. This concern for the inability of the photograph accurately to reflect Pound's image of himself, along with the same paranoia about being depicted as a Jew, is reproduced in another of Pound's exchanges with William Bird about Strater's initials for the *Cantos*: there Pound complains about Strater's representation of Sigismundo, who is the type of Pound's imaginary identifications: 'He has made Sidg into a Yid cousin of Seldes.'[8]

Pound, then, desires there to exist a reserved complementarity between himself and his image, and thereby denies any split between the agency of the eye and the procession of its gaze, a split which Lacan posits as a fundamental condition in the formation of the subject's relation to a founding lack, the 'manque-à-être'[9] which the castration anxiety institutes. The illusion of the idealist subject is, for Lacan, that of being a consciousness 'seeing itself seeing itself'[10] and so practicing the mastery of the eagle-eye. Pound's discomfort at not being able to see himself in his image is a symptom of the neurosis which is desperate to 'recreate a harmony with the real'.[11] It is hardly surprising, then, to find out Pound's alarm on seeing pictures of Joyce in 1916 (when he still thought to understand and admire Joyce's project), which plainly indicated that Joyce's eyesight was giving him trouble. Pound's concern with Joyce's eyes cannot be separated from his belief in the specular relationship I have been talking about: indeed, his manner of stressing his disappointment with Joyce's *work in progress* after *Ulysses* is to point out that Joyce's 'mind has been deprived of Joyce's eyesight for too long'.[12] Pound's increasing dissatisfaction with Joyce's writing approximately follows the course of Joyce's deepening ocular difficulties: in his own terms, Pound's fear for Joyce's 'pathological eyes' becomes justified when the novelist has to undergo a series of operations for increasingly severe attacks of glaucoma which leave his eyesight in a much impaired state. Indeed, during the writing of *Finnegans Wake* Joyce was afflicted with having to wear a patch over one eye and by a simultaneous decrease in the efficiency of the other eye which he described as 'my one bedazzled eye'.[13]

Pound himself reports that 'I had a rather alarming experience with my own eyes about ten years ago.'[14] The extent of the alarm that this must have provoked is indicated by his obtaining the most up-to-date information on opthalmic science then available and handing it to Joyce, urging him to get about correcting the problems as soon as possible. He even presumes to locate the precise nature of Joyce's ailment in a 'quasi-scientific diagnosis at a distance and on so little evidence', and he suspects the 'oculist of believing that your astigmatism is harmonic and not inharmonic' and so perhaps being capable of rectification without resort to surgery.

The cutting of the homogeneous body and especially of the privileged eye would, of course, be the apogee of horror to Pound: thus his admiration for Wyndham Lewis who, in old age, refused to undergo an operation that would put both his eyesight and his mental efficiency in jeopardy. 'Wyndham Lewis chose blindness/rather than have his mind stop' (794). This demonstrates that the necessary strength of mind and degree of perception in a genius, although mediated by the eye, was not for Pound totally dependent upon it but rather more on the homogeneity of the inside and outside of the organism. The eye, the meeting edge of man and the world, is the symbol and guarantee of the harmony of inside and out. Thus, the connection between eyesight and genius was quite important and clear in Pound's mind. This is demonstrated by his recommending to Joyce the same oculist as had treated him, George Gould. The oculist had written about the relation of eyesight and genius and was thus, as Forrest Read puts it, 'irresistible to Pound',[15] his principal recommendation being that 'He'd be interested in your work and from that in your eyes.' The preservation of Joyce's eyes thus becomes a purely literary matter: other opthalmic specialists would not be appropriate for treating Joyce since they 'are not, so far as I know, interested in literature'.[16]

Alarm that the very writer whom he had singled out as a remedy to the 'obstructionist and provincial' who constitute 'the permanent danger to civilization'[17] certainly led Pound to help Joyce as much as he possibly could. But in one of his letters, even while he praises Joyce's possession of the necessary eye, there exists a telling parapraxis from Pound which can be considered as the first of his doubts and the germ of his later discontent with Joyce's writing. Forrest Read transcribes the letter in question which was written on 9 February 1917, thus:[18]

God knows where you have been and what you have gazed upon with your [*crossout*: myopic] microscopic [*crossout*: eye] , remarkable eye.

In his mistake Pound betrays what is to become his fundamental objection to Joyce's work — its shortsightedness. In its etymology, the word 'myopic' refers to the shutting of the eye; Pound's use of it here thus explicitly attacks Joyce's concept of the 'nightynovel', the book of the time of shut-eye which deals with that part of human existence 'passed in a state which cannot be rendered sensible by the use of wideawake language, cutanddry grammar and goahead plot'.[19] Joyce's writing clearly moves into that area of Hell, the darkness that underlies the space where Pound has chosen to live and work — the ground of masculine control and enlightenment. In that locus the body is seen as unalterable, an undifferentiated site where control is imperative. Pound's fetishisation of the phallus and his attempted disavowal of castration and lack, and of the bodily effluxes that anality bespeaks, counter bodily loss in so far as any such loss is symbolic. It is certainly not by accident that he and Joyce established in their letters to each other a disagreement that is rendered in terms of the anus and the phallus. Pound objects to the 'cloacal labour' that Joyce embraces, and proclaims himself to be 'un peu plus phallique'.[20]

In some of his writing Pound claims that the anal/phallic polarity is simply expressed by the difference between prose and poetry. 'Most good prose arises, perhaps, from an instinct of negation; is the detailed, convincing analysis of something detestable; of *something one wants to eliminate.*' Poetry, on the other hand, should be conceived of as the expression of 'a positive, i.e. of desire' (LE 324n; my emphasis). It is clear enough by now that this involves precisely the paradox that Pound's work continually runs up against. His poetry is more exactly the articulation of the *repression of desire* through the agency of a positivity which, by its very reductive and imaginary nature, cannot embrace desire since desire always points to its founding in castration and anality and to the condition of separation of the body. Poetry, in Pound's view, should be the product of an 'emotional synthesis' and so it can be said to draw on to itself, tighten the exits of the body, tighten its idiom.

All this directly weighs upon Pound's chosen preference for what he calls the prose tradition in verse, and the concomitant analerotic representations that his work moves through. Good prose, it seems, should have the qualities that he was able to praise in Joyce's early work: the strength of *A Portrait of the Artist as a Young Man* is to treat the sordid 'with his metallic exactitude' (LE 412) or, in other words, to be able to treat the dirt as gold or money in the terms of the metaphoric alteration I have derived from Freud's work. Such an operation is at the very root of all true value in Pound's economic/literary system: as far as he is concerned *Finnegans Wake* represents devaluation and so 'has bout FLOWED long enuff': it is the diarrhoea of the 'flow of conSquishousness'.[21]

When Pound insists on his totalitarian synthesis he is effectively championing an art of the signified against an art of the signifier: some true value in terms of meaning must be assignable to the signifier. Joyce, 'who had administered the laxative bolus',[22] obviously threatened the tight unity of the relationship between signifier and signified that Pound so much desired to establish. Joyce's work is quite evidently inscribed at the level, as Lacan puts it, 'of the structure of the signifier, of the languages spoken in a stuttering, stumbling way'.[23] Joyce 'has sat within the grove of his thought, he has mumbled things to himself, he has heard his voice on the phonograph and thought of sound, sound, mumble, murmur'.[24] Or, as Joyce himself puts it, he has moved into that area where 'the brain uses the roots of vocables to make others from them which will be capable of naming its phantasms, its allegories, its allusions':[25] where one signifier means something only for another signifier in the chain of active *signifiance*.

The area of the unconscious, structured as a language, and its ever present murmur appear to Pound as a sort of drunkenness and lack of control: Joyce is 'too soused'[26] to be sure of inclusion in a list of the great living writers who could preserve civilisation. In this respect, Pound's always tolerant but sometimes strained relationship with William Carlos Williams might have recognised the existence of another anti-Poundian current in Williams's early desire to 'be free . . . to write, write as I alone should write, for the sheer drunkenness of it'.[27] Indeed, Williams's work often quite explicitly pleads for the recognition of materiality in art, against Pound's early repression of it: Williams continually reminds his reader that 'writing is made of words and nothing else'[28] and praises Joyce's Rabelaisian characteristics[29] which, as we have seen, Pound firmly relegates to the uncertain and untrustworthy area of puerility.

It is, then, a poetics of freedom that has to be set against Pound's, one for which the control over body and language gives way to some of the 'potentiel d'épanouissement, toutes les possibilités de la libération d'énergie' that Bataille advocates with his notion of the pineal eye.[30] Rather than a poetics of control and investment of power in the eye and phallus, Bataille suggests in his image of the volcanic, anal orifice at the top of the head a devaluation of those two instruments of control. In the pineal eye the clarity of vision so cherished by Pound and the sacred disseminating force of the phallus are both undone by 'les cris d'une éjaculation grandiose mais puante'.[31] The pineal eye is, finally, an anal orifice, liberated into the fun and opacity of its effluxes; it is 'un organe sexuel d'une sensibilité inouïe' (one, at least, to which Pound would turn a deaf ear) which opposes the homogeneity of man and his image.

If the notion of the pineal eye appears 'affreusement ridicule'[32] – which it undoubtedly would to Pound – Joyce can be said to be capable of enjoying its subversive pleasures. One of the little limericks that he would send to Pound in his letters both accepts and makes fun of Pound's aversion to his 'cloacal obsession':

> There once was a lounger named Stephen
> Whose youth was most odd and uneven.
>> He throve on the smell
>> Of a horrible hell
> That a Hottentot wouldn't believe in.[33]

In *Finnegans Wake* Joyce plays on Pound's continual insistence that to work 'Down where the asparagus grows'[34] is unaccepbble: when he refers to 'an Esra' in all his 'unbluffingly blurtuubruskbblunt' energy (FW 116), he is surely aware that the poet is there inscribed as the reverse of the producer of anal delights: Esra, arse in reverse, is the backward phallic champion, the Shaun figure of *Finnegans Wake*. An Esra would be antipathetic to the areas of Joycean production and unwilling to follow Stephen 'down as far as the lector most bloody benevolens can be expected to respire'.[35] Pound, of course, recognises the extent to which Joyce's prose attaches to the ridiculousness, the hilarity, that Bataille offers, but he maintains his 'gallic preference for Phallus' and claims to be aware that 'mittel europa humour runs to the other orifice'.[36]

It is in Mittel Europa that the adulteration of values and the establishment of a 'general indefinite wobble' (173) in civilisation seems to operate for Pound. In other words, he does not find that humour funny, and his own attempts to turn the direction of the humour have a definite humourless air about them. His exposure in 'Canto 35' of the Jew-influenced middle European life, 'rather like some internal organ/some communal life of the pancreas . . . sensitivity/without direction' (173), is rather baldly compared to the establishment of the Mantua *fontego* which was supposed to promote more precise values in economic life and thus in civilisation generally. His attempt to show that the 'century old joke on Italia/was now on someone else' (172) — that is, on the Europeans who have capitulated to Jewish practices where the Italians have not — is purely petty and mechanical. Furthermore, whatever humour there is in his caricatures of these people or his transcriptions of their accents (as in the 'tale of the perfect schnorrer: a peautiful chewisch poy' (174)) is absolutely bitter.

Jewishness, anal humour, Joyce's project of free-flowing discourse, drunkenness and so on all represent for Pound the Invidia, the evil eye which threatens the values of goodness and propriety. Invidia jeopardises the power of the oracular eye that presides over the beginnings of the American Revolution and over the tenets of Utopian idealism. Joyce's patch over his left eye and the reduced vision in the other eye condemns him, according to Pound, to a discourse which cannot be guaranteed, in the way that Pound's own expects to be, by the law of the father: no god presides over its beginnings. Whereas Pound can always claim to control desire by assuming the proprietorship of meaning in language, Joyce's language resists such control and allows itself free and hilarious play within the relational aspects of language where, as *Finnegans Wake* amply demonstrates, there is *literally* no end to meanings. In his acceptance of the separation of the language of the signifier from his own body Joyce is recognising the demands of the metonymic institution of lack, of desire. Joyce's language, doing without the mechanics of neurotic repression as we have seen them so integrally at work in Pound's view of things, approaches the more mobile language of the perverse.

The relative stances of Pound and Joyce can be quite conveniently summed up in terms suggested in the work of Julia Kristeva.[37] In setting the idea of the speaking subject with an identity fixed within a frame of a social institution which is recognised by that subject as the support for his identity, against the idea of a process that the speaking subject enjoins and is enjoined by in the actual articulation of that fixed position, Kristeva is led to posit a distinction between the activity of the *symbolic* structure of the first position and the *semiotic* of the second. The two continually cross, and meet with a certain excess in language. Together the symbolic, as a *structure*, and the semiotic, as a *process*, involve a constant production and generation of excess which is experienced by the speaking subject as pleasure (a sort of transgressive appreciation of excess). The radical heterogeneity that the crossing of the symbolic with the semiotic entails is opposed to the simple (Poundian) fixity of position that the bonding of signifier and signified entails. Poundian practice, described in Kristevan terms as an act of *signification*, is in opposition to the process of what she calls *signifiance*.

Pound's work is always concerned with *signification*, with the ideal coincidence of sign and meaning. Joyce is more concerned with the disrupting of that coincidence within the actual process, the theatre perhaps, of language. In Joyce's work there is no privileged discourse which can be used as the controller of all others. From his own transgressive desire to 'have seven tongues and put them all in my cheek at once'[38] we can derive a manifesto for his whole writing practice, from the weaving of differently derived discourses in 'Ivy Day in the Committee Room', where no indication of privileged dominance is given to any particular mode of discourse, through a similar sort of writing in the 'Cyclops' section of *Ulysses* where even (or especially) Bloom's discourse is upturned and ridiculed in the midst of others, through to *Finnegans Wake* with its absolute refusal of any readerly metalanguage and its offering of a continual process in language which leaves in its wake the erasure of the fixed subject of signification. Joyce's *parti pris* is for the continual and endless articulations of language as against the assumption of a fixed position of subjectivity. This can be termed otherwise as simply the decision to include the materiality of language itself in writing and to have it unmediated by the direct lines of vision that are supposedly the benevolent guide to Pound's activity. Joyce is for process against fixity, for language against sight.

(ii) Writing

It may well be that the whole movement of Joyce's work can be related to exactly that drunkenness that Pound suspects him of. Joyce was a well known drinker. On his trip to Scandinavia in 1936 he was struck by the Danish words for 'to work' and 'to order a glass of wine' (*at bestille nogel* and *at bestille en flaske vin*), saying that he was in Copenhagen to do both things.[39] In a similar playful vein in *Finnegans Wake* Joyce makes much of the name of his favourite wine, a Swiss wine called Fendant de Sion. Joyce's picture of the anal writer, Shem the Penman, emphasises that 'his lowness creeped out first via foodstuffs' and that he was given to 'gulp down mmmmuch too mmmmany gourds' (FW 171) of Sion's (Shaun's: Shaun is Shem's counterpart brother and opposite in *Finnegans Wake*) wine. Richard Ellmann tells us how Joyce, when drinking this wine with Ottocaro Weiss, noted its likeness to urine: 'Orina. Si . . . ma di un'arciduchessa.'[40] It is this wine, made from grapes whose skin is split, that Shem drinks in celebration of bodily effluxes: it comes from 'a douches' (the gentle duchess's ablutions) although it 'snot her fault' (rather, the mucus which exudes from the fault in her skin) and is known in *Finnegans Wake* as 'Fanny Urinia': 'Any dog's quantity of it visibly oozed out thickly' from the drunken writer. It is exactly this scandalous flow that Pound abhors, abstemious himself, with his role as editor of the jakes scene in 'Calypso' being corroborative evidence of this.[41]

The mutiple meanings squeezed into just this simple fragment of *Finnegans Wake* are an example of Joyce's celebrated 'quadrivial' method. This is a method of writing that provides what Stephen Heath calls 'perpetual fragmentation'[42] in a 'collideorscape' concerned with the collision and rupture and escape (escapade) of meanings. Taking Joyce's hint to Robert Sage 'that Joyce's writings, from *Dubliners* to the present book [FW] form an indivisible whole',[43] it is necessary to find some of the same sort of effects of the method in earlier forms.

We might look at 'Ivy Day in the Committee Room' which concerns a group of Irish Republican canvassers at a low ebb in their campaigning and discussing it. Their different voices are overlayed one on top of the other to form a set of discourses 'suspended in a vacuum of sense'. What is missing, as Colin MacCabe has pointed out,[44] is precisely the controlling metadiscourse of classical prose writing — another voice which will make out for the reader the sense of the varied opinions and utterances of the gathered characters. If there is a controlling discourse it is one of absence, lack, most signally to be perceived in Joe Hynes's recitation of his ballad 'The Death of Parnell'. Parnell's absence has been pointed out earlier when Hynes stares at the ivy lapel on his coat and expresses the wish that Parnell were still alive. But even that discourse of absence is made ironical in the final line of the story with Mr Crofton agreeing that Hynes's ballad 'is a very fine piece of writing' (D 152). It is difficult not to feel that in those words the narrative voice is pointing as much to the story itself as to the ballad in a playfully ironical manner; noting, indeed, the very absence of a guaranteeing voice and the light of a metadiscourse which would normally be the voice to lay claim to any deliberation of value.

The absence of that light, as it gives way to the stasis of sense in the men's inconsequential conversation, has already been played with in the text by the fact that the scene begins entirely in the dark. Even the light of two flickering candles that O'Connor introduces points up the emptiness and lack of clarity in the scene: 'A denuded room came into view and the fire lost all its cheerful colour' (D 134/5). For Joyce, the light can offer no more than that. This story suggests, then, the vanity of that light, its illusion of being able to control and direct the language and opinion or the variation in people's discourse. The emphasis in this story is on the writing, not on what is unfolded to the sight — not on vision.

Joyce's strategic overlay of discourses is present not only in *Dubliners* but throughout his entire work. The celebrated passage in *Portrait of the Artist as a Young Man*, where Stephen reflects with the dean on the word 'tundish', provides a simple example of the collision of discourses.[45] Stephen's general concern with the qualities of language and the transformations of his own name extend this reflection and mark the gap between the language he conceives and the meanings that it produces, or the gap between his consciousness and his ability to communicate. In the more complicated project of *Ulysses* Joyce collapses this question into the very procedures of his narrative: the short paragraph which begins 'Calypso' will indicate what I mean.

Mr Leopold Bloom ate with relish the inner organs of beasts and fowls. He liked giblet soup, nutty gizzards, a stuffed roast heart, liver slices fried with crustcrumbs, fried hencod's roes. Most of all he liked grilled mutton kidneys which gave to his palate a fine tang of faintly scented urine. (U1 57)

This paragraph plays with the difference between the narrative voice and Bloom's colloquial voice, and the gap between the 'nutty' materiality of Bloom's list of preferred food and the narrative's communication of that list in the phrase 'the inner organs of beasts and fowls'. The formality of that phrase, corroborated by the title of 'Mr' given to the object of the narrative voice, is undercut by the simple article in the next sentence, 'a'. The question of where that 'a' comes from is all-important. It is, in fact, over-determined: it has affinities with Bloom's interior voice – it seems to come from his musings – but also has affinities with any colloquial idiom to which the narrative voice might attach; yet it is from another register than the fine turns of the first and third sentences. Between those two sentences the actual materiality of the writing is allowed to emerge.

Dubliners repeats that insistence on language in a most definite reflexive manner. A telling example is the story of Mr Duffy and Mrs Sinico, 'A Painful Case'. There, the stasis and paralysis always evident and familiar in *Dubliners* appear to be the direct product of Duffy's unliberated hold on language. His is a position firmly entrenched in the symbolic (in Kristeva's sense) and it is traversed by the semiotic activity of Mrs Sinico. We are told of Duffy's reading habits, his 'auto-biographical habit which led him to compose in his mind from time to time a short sentence about himself containing a subject in the third person' (D 120). He sees Mrs Sinico's death on the railway lines as the debasement of his own linguistic proprieties. Reading about her death through the 'threadbare phrases' (D 128) of journalistic prose, he is revolted by 'the whole narrative of her death' and is depressed by the 'squalid tract of her vice' (which was nothing other than drunkenness). He finally feels that 'he sentenced her to death' (D 130). The memory of her is instilled in him by the noise of a train 'reiterating the syllables of her name' (D 131) with its pounding rhythm. The story seems to suggest that his ordered and controlled stance towards language – and we remember that he 'abhorred' in a very Poundian way 'anything which betokened physical or mental disorder' (D 120) – actually constitutes the painful case as it is summed up in his lonely and immobile position at the very end of the story. Mrs Sinco has tried to transcend the order of his constrained view of things; she has tried, in fact, to 'cross the line' (D 126) of his prosaic world, to produce a disturbance on the surface of his fixity.

As elsewhere in *Dubliners* all that seems to be able to produce that disturbance, that flaw, in the ordered body has something to do with music. The meetings that Duffy and Mrs Sinico stole from the stasis of their lives were presided over by their mutual love of music as it marked out the locus of their desires. In 'Clay' music acts as the indicator of release from the hygienic sterility of the lives of Joe and Maria. In 'Eveline', the playing of the street organ acts as promise of Eveline's supposedly imminent escape:'Down far in the avenue she could hear a street organ playing.' 'She knew the air' (D 41) as it prefigured, in Joyce's playful pun, her departure for the exotic land of Buenos Ayres, but she is finally unable to cross the line: she cannot bring herself to cross the iron railing that separates her from Frank and her desires. In 'The Dead' it is specifically the long chain of musical events in the Morkan household that releases the memory of Michael Furey, the fury of desire, into the lives of Gretta and Gabriel.

The place of musicality in Joyce's work can be seen, then, as precisely that of the materiality of language opening up the text by importing desire. If any vindication were needed of Joyce's perfect little verses it would reside in their almost 'triumphant evasion of substance' in their search for musical flow. Joyce's well-known fondness for sentimental songs is another mark of that desire, as is his conviction that the dislike of his later work in some quarters could be altered by the appearance of *Pomes Pennyeach*. This predilection for the passage of musicality through his texts is further emphasised by his behaviour while supervising the translations of *Finnegans Wake*. Richard Ellmann points out that time and again 'Joyce's great emphasis was upon the flow of the line, and he sometimes astonished [his translators] . . . by caring more for sound and rhythm than sense.'[46] Ellmann characterises this attitude towards sonority, rhythm and verbal play in his texts as a 'fine carelessness'[47] on Joyce's part, an unfaithfulness to the sense of the passages being translated. Yet that carelessness, like Joyce's propensity towards reckless spending, provides a profound indication of his aims in writing: in any case, faithfullness to the sense of any particular part of *Finnegans Wake* would first have to establish that such a dense piece of writing does in fact have a sense. All this, of course, is a far cry from Pound's attitude to the music of his texts. Pound, after starting his career by means of an exploitation of the music left to him by the poets of the nineteenth century and the troubadours, proceeded to simply *use* it, manipulate it, in the service of increasingly hectoring pronouncements. If this aspect of Joyce's work can be seen as a certain counterpoise to Pound's work, the poetry of Louis Zukofsky, which I will deal with in Chapter 7, might appear to use the revisionary example with a vengeance.

The project, in *Finnegans Wake*, of developing, as Ellmann puts it, 'his "storiella as she is syung" and not merely recorded',[48] involves an abandonment of writing to the signifier's drive and to the embracing of desire. The sighing of the song as it is sung is indicatively always present, from *Dubliners* on, as a procession of feminine sibilants and modulations. The female is specifically given in Joyce's writing as the bearer of an infinitude of meanings in language, as the locus of the semiotic, like Mrs Sinico. Far from being relegated, as in Pound's work, to the status of cipher of memory in language, she becomes the maker of meanings and their unattainable origin. She is nothing less than the endless run or flow or play of signifiers, based on the lack of the phallus which Pound is unable to come to terms with. If desire and language are constituted upon a lack then they both have no origin, no guaranteeing presence from which they can be said to be controllable. Joyce will exploit this, in the face of Poundian resentment.

The erasure of a fixed point of origin in language and in desire is perhaps best highlighted in *Ulysses* by Bloom's inscribing in the sand of the beach his message to Martha, a message which he can never complete and which is doomed to erasure. His first inscription is the phallic 'I' that marks his desire as it has been aroused and then dissipated by his adventure with Gerty MacDowell and by his thoughts of Molly and Martha. The phallic 'I' has been exhausted at the very moment of its writing: it becomes useless: 'Useless. Washed away' (U1 379) by the motive force of the sea. The rest of the inscription that he actually puts on to the sand is 'AM.A.' but 'Mr Bloom effaced the letters with his slow boot' and 'flung his wooden pen away'. The 'A' that he writes is the counterbalance to the phallic 'I': it is the mark of female desire, the beginning of the alphabet, or the 'allaphbed' (FW 18) from where life emerges.

The 'A' is also the sign of Anna Livia Plurabelle in *Finnegans Wake*, the 'isocelating biangle' (FW 165) whose geometry can be neither fixed nor learnt; it is, furthermore, the red triangle on that instrument of drunknenness, the bottle of Bass beer that appears to Bloom several times in his wanderings around Dublin (his fascination with advertising being ad-verted to it). In the Gold Cup 'Bass's mare', of course, is 'still running' (U1 324). Bass ale is brewed at Burton-on-Trent and so the sign turns our attention to Sir Richard Burton and his quest for the source of the River Nile. That search – for a nothingness (a nil), and an origin – epitomises the romantic assignation of origins to the sacred river Alph, which for Coleridge ran into a sunless sea. In the concluding section to *Finnegans Wake* we find 'Old Bruton' representing the nine-teenth-century British preoccupation for the 'Deepereras', engaging in 'mudden research' (FW 595) for that original place. The locating of what is but a symptom of that general romantic fascination with the origin, the place where the indecipherable letter has emerged from, acts as one of the major structural ploys – and one of the major jokes – in *Finnegans Wake*. The place that Joyce always offers as illusory, the fantasmic source of what is 'always passing, the stream of life' (U1 88), is the underground sacred sea to which ALP returns and from which she begins again 'along the riverrun' (FW 628 & 3).

Within the movement of Joyce's 'drama parapolylogic' (FW 474), it is Shem the Penman, the writer, who can become the 'malestream in seagulf' (FW 547), attaching to the plurality of desire. Bloom echoes this role in his uncertainty about phallic control – 'Who has the organ here I wonder' (U1 83) – and in his recognition of his own 'feminisible name' (FW 73). (The latter notion, perhaps, stems from Otto Weininger's book *Sex and Character*, which claimed that 'Jews are by nature womanly men',[49] and underlines that uncertainty.) In contrast to Shem is Shaun who makes the idealist gesture of trying to 'isolate i from my multiple mes' (FW 410), or from the mess of the writer's con-dition, and thus he demonstrates his support of the ideology of the law of the phallus, and his attachment to the control of the father who is claimed to be 'constantly the same as and equal to himself and magnifi-cently well worthy' (FW 32). In Irish politics as he knew them Joyce would have seen the imaginary identification with Parnell as another and dangerous symptom of this vindication of the paternal full subject; which is perhaps why Parnell figures in Joyce's major writing as no more than a symbolic absence, Joyce's own mind being abhorred by the repressive identifications that any nationalist politics encourage. The infallible subject of which Shaun is the type and supporter in *Finnegans Wake* can be related to exactly the mechanisms of the Poundian subject who is proposed as that sort of supposed identity. The Poundian struggle to attain to such an identity takes place within the context of the repression of anality and the disavowal of castration and is embodied in the Shaun figure with its counterpart in the projective abilities of Shem the Penman.

It must be noted, nevertheless, that Joyce's view of Shem and Shaun is as 'a daintical pair of accomplasses' (FW 295). The drives and characteristics of both are inscribed within the Earwicker family as a sort of collapsed Oedipal drama. The signal splitting of the word 'identical' into 'a daintical', apart from prefiguring a certain bisexuality in its dainty aspect (the two also become 'lasses'), and alluding to the Scandinavian origins of the Irish race, institutes a splitting of the subject's identity within himself and leaves precisely the gap, castration's lack, ironically embedded in the word 'identical', 'a-daintical'. The splitting of the subject is crucial to Joyce's work: the two accomplices are a pair (or a *père*, perhaps) in the production of the subject's lack as the two of them actually come to blows while trying to learn, in their role as compasses, to 'see figuratleavely the whome of your eternal geomater' (FW 296) in the geometry lesson. Their endeavours join figuratively in the ur-space of what the fig-leaf hides, exactly the homely gap of the mother's continual lack in her whom-ness.

As the brothers/sisters circle around that unknowable gap in a state of flux we can be reminded of Pound's geometry of mastery, the rose in the steel-dust where the lines of force are controlled by the central solidity of the magnet. In Joyce's counterpart diagram (Fig-leaf I), the pair of accomplices circle around the 'secret stripture' of ALP's eternal triangle, or her 'isocelating biangle'. They move around the mysterious gap of the mother's body and away from the phallic force of Pound's geometry in a way which denigrates the identity and origin seeking 'old Pantifox Sir Somebody Something Burtt' (FW 293). They encircle, in other words, the failure of paternal power, the power of which Earwicker is supposed to be able to avail himself and which Bloom discovers in the vacuum of the 'AM' that he writes on the beach enclosed by the opposite forces of the 'I' and the 'A'. Earwickers's power is questioned in the very transformation of his name to the inefficient 'her weaker' (FW 79), even amidst the proclamations of his phallic dominance: 'I perpetually kept my ouija ouija wicket up . . . I was firm with her' (FW 532 & 547) is how he attempts that revindicating claim. Yet such power is continually calumnied, doubted and seen through in *Finnegans Wake*: 'Finn again's weak' (FW 93). Even in its genitival capacities it is doubted. Stephen has already decided in *Ulysses* that 'Paternity may be a legal fiction' and that it is from one's mother that one learns 'how to bring thoughts into the world' (U1 207). His point of view is echoed by Bloom's own doubts about being able to attach any certainty to the fact or the moment of his fathering of Rudy, and his general musings on 'How life begins' (U1 90). His own penis, potentially the 'father of thousands' is, like his name, feminisible and seen as 'a languid floating flower' (U1 88).

The whole complex about bringing things into the world – children, thoughts, language, the subject – has been identified by Stephen Heath's very thorough work[50] on the single question that appears in *Finnegans Wake* and appears to haunt Joyce's writing: 'Where did thots come from?' (FW 597). That question brings into play, alludes to, the unending problem of the question of origin as the word 'thots' can be read as 'tots', children; imputes a notion of differentiation in the subject and his sexuality in 'th'autre(s)', the other; refers to the female sex by means of the Gaelic 'toth' and to the male sex in its 'that', the French *ça* of the penis; refers to the origin of language by reference to the god 'Thoth' who is the copyist and transmitter of the imperial language of Ra. This single question acts as a sort of summing-up of any number of the questions that Bloom poses himself and the universe – questions of subjectivity, sexuality, the production of life, the dissemination of language and writing. A few of Bloom's questions:

What is she? (U1 289)

Why have women such eyes of witchery? (U1 346) (Of which-ery)

Tell me who made the world. (U1 159) (We recall Bloom's continual play with the opposition world/word which is provoked by Martha's letter.)

What do they love? Another themselves? (U1 377) (A question relating to Freud's 'Was will das Weib?', and a further interrogation of identity.)

Why me? (U1 377) (Or why AM I A?)

Who's getting it up? (U1 76) (Who has the phallus?)

Who has the organ here I wonder. (U1 83)

Got the horn or what? (U1 266)

What kind of voice is it? (U1 83) (A question of voice and the production of language by the subject.)

Who is this wrote. (U1 277) (What is the origin of writing?)

Where do they get the money? (U1 367) (A question which relates in a complicated way to Bloom's musings on the value of women as in 'Nausicaa': 'Suppose he gave her money ... She's worth ten, fifteen, more a pound ... All that for nothing' or for the access to the source of the Nile, the nil, the lack. (U1 367))

Such reiterated interrogation is also echoed by and enters into harmony with other questions in *Ulysses*: Stephen's 'Who is the father of any son?' (U1 207) and his 'What's in a name?' (U1 209), Miss

Douce's 'Aren't men frightful idiots?' (U1 256), and even Terry the
Barman's 'Who won?' the big race (U1 324), the answer to which is
not the phallic 'Sceptre' — 'Frailty, thy name is Sceptre' — but the
complete outsider, 'Throwaway' — a sort of nominal metonymy for
anal rubbish.

I list some of these questions merely to let them reverberate with
the question that Heath has dealt with in a strategy that he shares with
other critics like Frances Bolderoff who stresses the structural importance of the Bloom-like riddle in *Finnegans Wake*, 'why do I am alook
alike a poss of porterpease?'[51] This too is another question of identity
to which the book itself acts as a sort of polyvalent non-answer. Much
more: in a sense *Finnegans Wake* has itself constituted a question, one
addressed to the writing that it is not, but which it yet includes. For
many critics, and for Pound and a large section of the reading public,
Finnegans Wake is to be answered by endless and nervous periphrasi-
sation or by blank response — a peculiarly apposite fate for a book
whose infinitude passes precisely through nothingness, through the spaces
of lack and insufficiency as they constitute the endless run of desire.

It is Bloom who offers the mode of reading appropriate to this book
which is the unanswerable and unswervable question. His own uncertainty and inability to get to the bottom of things (his negative capabilities, if one will) encourage the linking and continual reproductions of
all the questions. Bloom himself advocates that we 'read it nearer' (U1
61). Reading should no longer consist in the passive assumption of a
fixed position controlled by the classic metadiscourse that can be traced
back to a constraining and sermonising author: paternity and authorship
are the same fiction and both go to constitute the 'soft subject gaze at
rest' (U1 161) so that the reader can receive, as if dropped from above,
the instructions and documents of an author infallibly identical to himself and who encourages and demands the co-opting and co-operative
fixity of the reader. Reading should rather consist in the wandering and
effusive acceptance of the erasure of origin and the celebration of the
effluxes, the discourse of the body.

Bloom's own reading of 'Matcham's Masterstroke' behind the 'crazy
door of the jakes', 'above his own rising smell' (U1 70 & 71) in the
process of defecating can act as a sign of the anal/phallic tensions
between Joyce's writing and that of Pound. The latter, of course, tried
to suppress the references to the act of defecation as it implicitly fragments and undoes the story in which 'Matcham often thinks of the
masterstroke by which he won the laughing witch who now' (U1 71).
Matcham, with the drama of the subject's competition against the law of

the father inscribed in his very name, exercises by the mastering stroke of his own revindicated phallus the control over threatening female desire, over the laughing witch who becomes ALP; this is the very course of the Poundian subject. Joyce's work, accepting as it does the workings of desire, and mocking phallic control, takes writing laughingly to 'list, as she bibs us, by the waters of babalong' (FW 103). Even there, if we remember Pound's refusal or denial of the efficacy of childish recollections, is inscribed in the flowing, Babylonian, babbling baby language a laughing resistance to Pound's poetics.

(iii) Politics

Given that the standard critical and biographical work on Joyce indicates that his political stance is one of pure individualism, and given his own aversion to the practice of psychoanalysis, it may at first appear gratuitous and foolhardy to base on his work the initial furtherance of my particular reading of a possible revision of Poundian poetics. I hope that my readings so far do not allow such doubts much purchase, but in any case the situation with Joyce is not so clear cut as his critics might have us believe. The fact that Joyce appeared in his lifetime to be 'a resolute neutral in politics'[52] and that his texts refuse to give themselves to a particular party-political stance becomes irrelevant in the light of his linguistic practice: if Pound's language is inherently Fascistic, then my juxtaposition of Pound and Joyce (indeed, a juxtaposition suggested by their own view of each other) would indicate that Joyce's strategies are implicitly anti-Fascist. As Colin MacCabe tells us, the 'political question for any text is not whether the text "contains" the correct political line as part of its content':[53] it is more a question of what particular texts suggest in their attitude towards, and use of, language. Pound indulges in just that — a specific *use* of language to establish and promulgate the sort of epistemological relations that I described when talking of, for instance, 'Canto 99'. Joyce's case is less simple.

James Joyce's writing attacks or countermands the notion of the unified subject engaged in the illusory activity of seeing himself seeing himself and being obsessed with meaning as a structure that can be transferred with minimum loss to the reader. In taking a stance against that Poundian method which is redolent of control and fixity, Joyce attaches his writing to the logic of the signifier outside of the fixed and juridical relations that make communications a purely legal fiction.

That position, precisely on the outside as Bloom is an outsider in the systems of exchange and communication which operated in Dublin society, becomes the locus specifically of desire and writing set against the strictures of communication.[54] Joyce's is what we might call a writing of uprootedness, of wandering (of Bloom's wondering), and of flow. And for Joyce the fixities of political identifications are firmly entrenched in the ideology of communication. The vacuity that he recognises there is perhaps nowhere more readily accessible than in 'Ivy Day in the Committee Room' or in 'Cyclops'. These pieces of writing have much in common in that they act as exemplary explorations of the possibility of disrupting the trammels of positionality and as indications of the freedom of writing.

It is both necessary and unfortunate that Joyce produced his major work at a time when both intellectuals and writers, not to mention the reading public, were demanding writing — perhaps of Pound's variety — which could place itself firmly and unequivocally in the public domain and demonstrate an understanding of the great political and social problems of the twenties and thirties: necessary because Joyce saw very clearly the illusions and subsequent dangers of that whole system of exchange and communication, and that whatever the merits or demerits of any particular party line the only real way out was a radical break with the ideology that held (and holds) such systems in position; unfortunate because he condemned himself to exile in the sense of not having an audience, since his work produced antagonism in the Fascists like Pound, in the liberals like Paul Léon who saw *Finnegans Wake* as a possible instrument of sabotage against left-wing aspirations because it might be construed as art written 'in the service of capitalist art accessible only to the idle few and rich',[55] and among the politically wary and weary such as Richard Aldington who could only see, 'beneath a veil, not of profundity but of emptiness', that Joyce had nothing to say to people in the upheavals of the inter-war years.[56]

It is indicative of the mood of those decades that, as Sylvia Beach saw it, 'the tendency in England at the time Joyce was beginning his new work was to keep the language within bounds'.[57] She is referring of course to the work of C.K. Ogden and his Basic English, an attempt to reduce the language to a set of indispensable words: a far cry from Joyce's own project of expanding the area of difference and desire in language. It is important to see Joyce's work in such a climate as a profound and yet solo revolutionary gesture, specifically situated on the margins of the ideology of political and social action that seemed to be shared by all the people he came into contact with. Harriet Shaw

Weaver seems to have been almost an exception to that rule. It is fairly apparent from her biography that her attachment to Joyce, his family and his work, and her rigorous encouragement, delayed her from involving herself with precisely the sort of political action for which Joyce could see no use. Weaver's 'long-standing socialist convictions'[58] were put into action in the thirties with the Labour and Communist parties in London only after her dealings with Joyce had come to a close. He, for his part, 'refused to take her seriously'[59] in the activities of her political life. Even the aid that he reputedly gave to several refugees from Fascism in the thirties does little to redeem him from the common charge of indifference to the political struggle. What occupied him totally was the political gesture that *Finnegans Wake* constitutes.

The episode in *Finnegans Wake* where Dolph, a transmutation of the Shem figure, tries to convince Kev, the Shaun figure of this instance, of the inefficacy and pathetic illusions of the father, involves itself with mocking the paradigms of the full subject in both sexual and political terms. Kev apparently strikes Dolph when he mocks the Irish nation-alist heroes Danny (O'Connell), Parnell and Connolly, and after he has mocked the father's weakness — 'How diesmal he was lying low' (FW 301): these amount to one and the same attack. Dolph has also been trying to make Kev accept the fact of the lack beneath ALP's skirts, 'to see figuratleavely the whome of your eternal geomater'. Kev's pref-erence for the power of the father will not face up to that lack. His answer is to fight physically with Dolph, like the political animal he is, instead of learning how to 'fight our Same' (FW 300) or see through the illusions of the full subject in both its political and sexual roles. Joyce's own political struggle is embedded in this passage: when the protag-onists of political life want to fight it out, he wants to try to deflect them from the system of imaginary identifications which make them do so. Thus, to paraphrase one of Joyce's comments about his work, *Finnegans Wake* may be tiresome and vulnerable to criticism of its commitment, but it was the only book he could have written to achieve that aim in the context of the sexual relations inscribed beneath polit-ical action.[60]

It is because Joyce brings into play those sexual questions and be-cause he specifically relates them to their outcrops in political life that it becomes justifiable to take in less than earnest his comments about psychoanalysis. As Bryher remarks, 'You could not have escaped Freud in the literary world of that time'[61] and to some extent his work and reputation were at the mercy of the vagaries and idiosyncrasies of fashionability. But Joyce was mostly wary of the actual practice of psychoanalysis rather than to its basic claims. In an interview with Djuna Barnes in 1922 Joyce implicitly links his work with Freud by claiming that it records 'what seeing, thinking, saying does to what you Freudians call the subconscious'; but in the same interview he rejects the analytic situation as being 'neither more nor less than blackmail'.[62] In keeping with his view of the two great protagonists of psychoanalysis, Freud and Jung, as a complementary pair — the Tweedledum and Tweedledee of the discipline — Joyce was pleased to hear that his intuitions into female psychology in 'Penelope' seemed to have taught Jung a lot, and yet he was vehemently opposed to the idea of undergoing analysis with the great doctor.[63]

None the less, Joyce seems to accept that the individual subject has 'something inside of me talking to myself' (FW 522) while still insisting that in his way he could 'psoakoonaloose myself any time I want'. Furthermore, Joyce was always mindful that his name was accidentally the same as a translation of Freud's name — exactly the sort of coincidence that Joyce thought to be meaningful.[64] Some part, then, of the thought of psychoanalysis, even by his own admission, remains relevant to Joyce's project. The writer who raises so many questions about the sexual identity of the subject as it is related to language would, however much he was repulsed by the idea of the analytic couch, never have gone so far as Pound in his rejection of psychoanalysis. Pound's comment that psychoanalysing people's 'in'nards which are merely the result of economic pressure' is just a 'lot of psychic bellyache' is followed up by the comment that 'J.J. drunk no more dam interest than anyone else' (Letters 52/3). Pound's recommendation that we 'at any rate buggar the castration complex' (Letters 268) would, I hope, have made Joyce laugh.

6 WOUNDED WOMAN: H.D.'S POST-IMAGIST WRITING

Have felt yr/vile Freud all bunk/
... You got into the wrong pig stye, ma chère;
EP to H.D.

In my dream Freud restores my faith. 'If I
had known Ezra, I could have made him alright,'
he says.
H.D.[1]

One of the most signal events in the history of twentieth-century poetry took place in a tea-room near the British Museum in September 1912. Ezra Pound, newly appointed 'foreign correspondent' to Harriet Monroe's *Poetry*, made corrections to some poems by Hilda Doolittle and, before sending them off for publication, signed them 'H.D., Imagiste'.[2] Hilda Doolittle, succumbing to what I have characterised as the essential Imagist procedure, thus became truncated, her name shortened to the simple siglum of Pound's suggestion. That inscription of the letters of her name has remained her publishable title; the epithet attached has also to a large extent rested with her, despite the removal of her work from the concise Imagism approved by Pound towards longer poems less marked by the lapidary economy and chiselled immediacy of the Imagists. These moments in the tea-room are indicative of Pound's very *mark* on twentieth-century verse, and the red pencil strokes that he makes typify his effective prescriptions. H.D.'s consequent struggle in her own writing with the impact of this event might perhaps be seen as an emblem of the difficulty and necessity involved in writing across the structures of Pound's presence.

As a sort of Mrs Sinico to Ezra Pound's Duffy, H.D. is ideally located to help explore some of the difficulties that Pound and his work leave us with. And this is not least because of the fact that she is a woman and so has necessarily to counter the imposition of Pound's ultimately phallocratic view of the individual subject and of writing. In the following discussion I intend to propose H.D.'s work, especially in its later phases, as an attempt, at least, to write a way out of the light and shadow of Pound's creativity. The story of that attempt will be symptomatic — more or less overtly — of the problems and concerns that any feminist writing has to deal with. In H.D.'s case, the whole project is the journey from Pound's truncation of her name towards the writing of her final work, *Hermetic Definition*, nearly fifty years later, where those initials become, as it were, re-fleshed, refreshed.

H.D's working-out of her relations with Pound have a privileged articulation in *End to Torment*, a memoir of Pound written in 1958 which proceeds by way of exploring H.D.'s personal relationship with Pound and offers interesting insights for the consideration of the general tensions of her writing. It was in April of 1958, attended by much indignation and sentiment and amid much general debate about the morality of poetry and its politics, that Pound was released from St Elizabeths. His case received extensive public airing and caused a certain perturbation. H.D. was among his supporters who, in the months leading up to his release, were anxious with him. She herself was in a sanatorium at Küsnacht, Switzerland, recovering from a debilitating fall. It seems to have been at the encouragement of her friend and doctor there, Erich Heydt the psychiatrist, that H.D. embarked upon this memoir of Pound. She had, furthermore, been spurred into reminiscence by what another friend, Norman Holmes Pearson (later her literary executor) chose to think of as Pound's 'end to torment' (ET 41). Pearson's phrase, as the final title of the piece, serves to reflect ironically not only Pound's situation at the time — Pound himself found the title 'optimistic' (ET xi)— but H.D.'s own. For many years she had resisted this working out of her links with Pound and their former engagement because of the pain inflicted by those memories: the end to her torment would seem to reside in the actual writing of these memories, in the painful excision or exorcism of Pound.

Pound had abandoned H.D. to go to Europe after they had been, apparently, engaged in Pennsylvania at the turn of the century.[3] In freeing himself from their liaison he seems to have done her considerable harm. It is precisely the wound he caused, the mark he inflicted, that is re-inflicted in the inscription 'H.D., Imagiste' at the bottom of a typed sheet, now slashed with 'his creative pencil' (ET 40), and that *End to Torment*, in the name of therapy, finally approaches squarely. During the writing, Pearson tells H.D. that it must be 'good not to be hiding something' (ET 41), and Heydt is seen almost to bully H.D. into resuscitating her memories. The two act in their instigatory roles almost as counterparts to Pound himself, repeating the sort of power over her creativity that the poet himself embodies. In the face of H.D.'s relief at being able to end the 'black out' (ET 26) that she had imposed on her memories of Pound, her long-delayed speaking out has finally a double edge in that it not only ends the torment of that 'hiding' but also registers the very mark that Pound had bequeathed her.

To meditate upon the effect of Pound's influence is, for H.D., to come to terms with the feeling that 'consciously or unconsciously, it seems that we have been bound up with him, bound up with him and his fate' (ET 37). The 'we' of her remark can be taken to read not only H.D. or her immediate circle, but also all those involved with the condition of writing in the twentieth century. Pound exercises both an actual and a metaphorical gaze on all that. Indeed, *End to Torment* begins with the influence of his actual eyes and their power. Despite their constituting 'his least impressive features' (ET 3), their pebble-like qualities and their coldness are capable of discharging 'Some kind of rigor mortis'. That propensity is explicitly patriarchal in H.D.'s text since she recognises that 'to recall Ezra is to recall my father' (ET 48). Charles Doolittle[4] was a professor of astronomy, first at the appropriately named LeHigh University and then at the even more apposite Sayre Observatory. It may be his qualities as a seer —and H.D. remembers him as always distracted, looking into space — that led to his identification with Pound (or at least was one of the many elements in the determination of that identification). But it is also his coldness: 'there is an icy chill in the air . . . frost in the air' (TF 27) when he exerts his paternal authority.

That cold authority is brought to bear when, signally enough, H.D. and her brother are caught playing with fire, setting light to some paper with their father's magnifying glass that had been stolen from his collection of sacred objects in his study (TF 21). The frostiness experienced then appears explicitly throughout H.D.'s work as a sign of the stamping of paternal authority. In 'Advent', an account of some of her analysis with Freud, H.D. remembers that Freud tells her that her father must have been a very cold man (TF 136). In this sense Pound's image is determined somewhat by his ability to re-install paternal domination. Yet Pound also acts as the emblem of creative, poetic power. That double condition is inscribed upon his very body, since not only does he have those cold eyes and 'snow on his beard' (ET 3), but he is endowed with a head of fiery red hair. The polarity, then, of fire and ice, of paternal authority and creativity, derives immediately from Pound's body and acts as part of one of the basic oxymora upon which much of H.D.'s work builds.

Against the cold of her father in her memory, that 'frozen' feeling of being the object of her schoolfriends' prurient gaze (ET 55), or the way in which Balzac's ambiguously sexed being in *Séraphita* dies in the snow, are set images of fire and warmth: the 'fiery moment incarnate' of seeing her fantasised son on a station bench (ET 33), the 'flaming virtuoso' piano playing of Van Cliburn (ET 50), and the 'Divine Fire' of May Sinclair's book of the same name which H.D. and Pound read together (ET 9/10). The same antithesis rises forcefully once again in H.D's account of a meeting with Pound in Venice in 1913: she contrasts the fiery heat of the air outside with her memory of the interior of Santa Maria dei Miracoli which is 'cool with a balcony of icy mermaids' (ET 6).

This fire of creativity, as antidote to its antithesis in coldness, induces a state of incapacitated and dominated femininity in H.D. Pound is the threatening and auspicious bearer of both forces. It is with him that H.D. had once before experienced 'the perfection of the fiery moment' when they were courting (ET 11), but that sensation exaggerates the feeling of its opposite. Since Pound had left her, the question of how that fiery moment can be sustained inevitably arises. It is, finally, the question of desire, of the sheer impossibility of being reinstated into that perfect state. That Pound is the locus of that impossibility is the realisation that *End to Torment* arrives at. H.D.'s 'hope of recalling Ezra' (ET 34) − in the sense of having him reconstituted before her − is finally renounced. The text of that realisation and renunciation moves from the facial image of Ezra on the first page (where he embodies the antitheses of restrictive authority and liberated creativity) to 'the bon-voyage letter that I sent [him] through Norman, [which] would not have reached [him] in time' (ET 61). In a sense that letter stays with H.D., marking the impossibility of achieving the end of desire through the male body which ends up departing. It would be easy to regard the memoir in terms of, as H.D. suggests, Solveig's final embrace given in loving but wounded resignation to the exhausted and beaten Peer Gynt after she has waited, 'spinning and weaving' − writing, perhaps − like Penelope (ET 20) waiting for the return of her lover, for the end to her torment. But 'no, this is something different': *End to Torment* is not the consolation of a waiting and faithful mother-wife, nor the resting place for the errant son-lover. H.D.'s project is always something other than that: she is the questing Isis, and Pound the prototypical object of her 'life-long Isis search' (ET 32), the type of the dismembered lover whose limbs must be recollected and laid to rest.

The element of collecting together the fragments of the Osiris body is quite apparent in H.D.'s bringing together the figures of different men in her life — Pound and her father and Heydt, for example. Another important figure (perhaps in some ways the most important) in that collocation is Sigmund Freud, the 'Professor' as H.D. calls him in an obvious recollection of Professor Doolittle. The objects and topography of her father's hallowed study compare in mystique to Freud's office where H.D. takes to the couch. But Freud is the ideal father: H.D. knows that 'my father possessed sacred symbols' (TF 25) and she goes to Freud in the hope and expectation that he can hand over to her the knowledge that will enable her to understand those symbols and thus discover the secrets of her paternal relationship.

Freud, then, was expected to 'give H.D. back the understanding that leads to victory'[5] or to the accession to creative knowledge which seemed to be the property of men: Pound owned it in his *Cantos*, her father had it in his seemingly hieroglyphic mathematical knowledge and the mysterious objects in his study, Freud had it in his intuitive power and ability to explicate the depths of the mind's involucrum, as well as in the classical objects and treasures he surrounded himself with. In any case, the power was always invested in some object which could be given to H.D., either actually or metaphorically.

It is by use of one of his invested objects that Freud marks his exploration of H.D.'s relation with these multiple fathers, and so with her mother. In *Tribute to Freud*, H.D. tells how Freud almost flaunted before her a figurine of Pallas Athene:

> *This* is my favourite,' he said. He held the object toward me. I took it in my hand. It was a little bronze statue, helmeted, clothed to the foot in a carved robe with the upper incised chiton or peplum. One hand was extended as if holding a staff or rod. 'She is perfect,' he said, *'only she has lost her spear.'* I did not say anything. He knew that I loved Greece. He knew that I loved Hellas. I stood looking at Pallas Athene. (TF 68/9)

Athene and Greece (Hellas) were important identificatory symbols for H.D. whose mother was named Helen: Athene and her winged attribute Nike (Victory) symbolised the possibility of overcoming obstacles and of unity with her mother and thus with a satisfying production of texts in her mother-tongue. Those symbolic functions are further determined by the fact that at school 'when I was seven, it was a Miss Helen who read us "Tanglewood Tales" ', a popular children's version of the classical mythology (TF 186-7).

The Greek connection is what H.D. clearly felt comfortable with and finally drew from Freud's presentation of the statuette. However, the fact that she italicised in her text the words 'only she has lost her spear' is an indication of the fact that she apparently understood what Freud was getting at – namely, her own lack of a spear, her own lack of a penis. Even in the apparently naive reporting that 'he held the object toward me. I took it in my hand' that knowledge is inscribed. It is easy to read, in fact, throughout H.D.'s work, the activities of the *Penisneid* that Freud wished to demonstrate to her. *End to Torment*, for example, describes the male-child that she imagines as a product of her love for Pound as 'a small yet sturdy male object' (ET 33). There can be little doubt (*pace* the many feminists who write against any such suggestion) that this 'Idol', the 'Wunderkind', up till now 'somehow hidden' (ET 51) is the symbol for the lost penis; it is, quite literally, the embodiment of H.D.'s unfulfilled desire for the lover who always leaves, and for her father, the 'aloof, distant' astronomer (TF 27). The fantasy child, complete with Pound's blazing red hair, is the fiery moment incarnate, a major signifier in what Freud saw as H.D.'s penis-envy.

The desire for that child, that symbolic penis, is fully apparent in H.D.'s determination that 'If I was not the Child, as I obviously was not (as a child), I would have the Child' (ET 51). In other words, in accordance with Freudian theory, on finding that her mother (to whom 'one can never get near enough' (TF 33)) 'likes my brother better' (TF 33) because of his superior ability to be the phallus for her mother's desire, the girl realises she cannot be *the* Child, the male-child. In resentment she turns to her father (and, after all, 'there are things, not altogether negligible, to be said for *him*' (TF 34)) with the desire to encompass his penis and keep it inside her body, eventually slipping, in Freud's words, 'along the lines of a symbolic equation – from the penis to the baby'.[6]

It is precisely, then, H.D.'s relation to the lost object that Freud attempts to make apparent to her, situating her firmly in the Oedipal drama as he saw it. His determined attitude towards her *Penisneid* is quite clear in the remark that H.D. remembers in 'Advent': commenting on her grandfather giving the young girl a lighted candle at a traditional Christmas Eve ceremony, Freud opines that 'if every child had a lighted candle given . . . we should have no more problems' (TF 124). The giving of a literal candle to H.D. goes towards reinforcing the recurring need for the symbolic penis, a need which she was trying to satisfy by means of her very contact with the Professor: she wished to take from him the knowledge just as she had taken her names from her father and from Pound. That knowledge is symbolised in the objects of Freud's office as they recall the power that resided in her father's room. Of all those perhaps the most telling are the magnifiying glass (with which, as H.D. terrifiedly but avidly watched, her brother demonstrated his phallic rivalry with his father) and the paper-knife that her father left her (TF 34). It is clear that the release of the feminine from the condition of cold unanimated subjectivity seems to depend for H.D. on the object, lost and then given back by the male.

The paper-knife is an especially privileged object: it not only acts as the symbol for the penis, but it also re-presents the phallic power of cutting and castrating. The knife is to fill the gap of castration, its wound, but also to be the reminder of castration through its ability to cut: it would provide the means for H.D. to be her father's son and yet it also registers, in its very role as a symbol, the female lack. It acts, in other words, as a vindicatory emblem of the law of the father.

The whole notion of *Penisneid* has been hotly debated and resisted by feminists and often used as a stick with which to beat Freud, since it can be construed as positing an intrinsic anatomical and thus psychical inferiority in women. It is possible, however, to see the girl's registration of the complex of castration as a representative of a more primary loss. The cutting that occurs when the child no longer sees itself as an undifferentiated mass or as totality and truth is the moment of Lacan's mirror-stage where the split condition of the child's imaginary relation to itself and the world is instituted.[7] That loss of wholeness may in its turn be related to a pre-ontological loss, the removal of the child from the womb, but in any case it is a loss that is always re-presented to the child in the castration anxiety and in the process of weaning. Lacan, following on from Freud's description of the *fort/da* game, where the child associates the power to make an object appear and disappear with the different sounds of the words *fort* and *da*, locates here the access to the symbolic and the relation of the cutting – the letter, he calls it – to the field of the symbolic. The game is concerned with reproducing symbolically the coming and going of the mother. The object that is moved, insignificant in itself, is to be associated by language with the coming and going, the presence and absence of the mother. Thus the child's language comes to connote

the up until then indissoluble link between presence and absence: if presence cannot assume any value except on the bedrock of absence, that is because something has been irremediably lost – precisely, absolute presence. *Thus the symbol emerges from a loss.*[8]

For H.D. the original loss as it is constantly re-presented can be substituted for, to a certain point, by the oblativity of the male. More importantly, and beyond that, the very activity of writing is born in the continual attempt to come to terms with the mark of loss, the letter, within the endless run of desire which is, quite literally, 'pourvu d'un objet'.[9] 'Deprived of an object' situates quite well the case of the letter which is the trace of the difference and loss that the *fort/da* game rests upon; or it is the mark of the gap which is opened up with the accession to the symbolic. Lacan also suggests that the mark that the letter constitutes is an incidence of the name of the father,[10] an idea that is taken up in Serge Leclaire's notion of the letter. Leclaire sees the letter as the bodily mark of both access and limit to desire: the subject is called upon 'to instigate that disappearance of self constituted by pleasure, but at the same time to conceal that anulment'.[11] In the case of H.D. the attempt to control that disappearance of self into the realm of metonymic desire is undertaken by submission to the representative of the paternal law. Inscribed upon that attempt is what she herself recognises as 'some form of prenatal fantasy' (TF 168): such a fantasy is a clear nostalgia for the mother, Helen/Hellas, or for 'the transcendental feeling of two globes . . . or the two transparent half-globes enclosing me'.

It is apparent that within this overlaying of identifications, in the double inscription of the letter that both avows and denies desire, we are dealing with similar materials as were at play in the articulations of Pound's relation to mother and father. But whereas with Pound there appeared to be a continual effort towards the disavowal of the cut, in H.D.'s work there is always an overt recognition of it and an equivocal tension. In the sense that H.D. attempts to explore the linguistic movements of presence and absence, of the name-of the father and of the maternal 'oceanic' feeling, she is writing against the stasis of Pound's poetics which is inscribed in the domain of disavowal and of vindicating paternal law. I shall show that, except for certain important points of articulation, H.D.'s work is finally given over to a notion of transcendent masculine power; however, what seems to me important about her work is its exploration of the tensions in the passage of the letter, and the fact that this exploration is undertaken in the shadow of Pound's paternalistic influence. H.D.'s writing can in this way be emblemised by *End to Torment* which indicates the need and desire for a semiotic crossing not only of the structures of Pound's work but also through his body and personality: in other words, H.D. undertakes a traversal of the Poundian *corpus*.

It is precisely the play of presence and absence that is arrayed at the heart of 'the polarities and oxymora from which her poetry builds'.[12] One of these oxymora I have already had the opportunity to deal with, namely the distinction between the cold and the fiery moment. Others are developed throughout H.D.'s work and include a fascination with the question of an absence mitigated by the presence of a speaking voice. This is one of the primary concerns of the poems in *By Avon River*, 'Good Friend', and of *Helen in Egypt* (particularly the last section, 'Eidolon'). In 'Good Friend' we meet Claribel, the absent princess who is mentioned twice in Shakespeare's *Tempest*:

> She is not there at all, but Claribel,
> Claribel, the birds shrill, Claribel,
> Claribel echoes from this rainbow-shell.[13]

Although absent she has a present voice. It turns out that the presence and the voice are bestowed upon her in much the same way as H.D. herself was endowed and formed by the slashing action of Pound's creative pencil:

> I only threw a shadow
> On his page,
> Yet I was his,
> He spoke my name;
>
> He hesitated,
> Raised his quill,
> Which passed,
> Waited a moment,
>
> And then fell
> Upon the unblotted line;
> I was born,
> Claribel.[14]

It is specifically by means of masculine action that the voice is given to the female: before that gift 'I had no voice.'[15] And here, too, we see the admission of the woman to the superior male that 'Sir, I am nothing but a name':[16] even when the power of utterance has been donated, still the woman defers to the creativity in the realm of the father. The whole movement of this in H.D.'s work can be summed up by the admissions of the following:

> I was dead
> and you woke me,
> now you are gone,
> I am dead.[17]

Yet, while there is a general recognition of the double-inscription of the letter in H.D.'s early work, it seems that it was her analysis with Freud that pointed the way from texts like *By Avon River* and *Red Roses for Bronze* where woman's identity is given to her by masculine presence, towards a later reworking of the letter's metonymic course. There are special moments in texts like *Hermetic Definition* or *Trilogy* where there is a refusal finally to hand over control to a masculine agency — be it the father, or the god-father, Amen, Zeus, whatever — but generally these books do actually devolve upon a recognition of some specifically male agency. The text which does, however, largely refuse such an offering is *Helen in Egypt*, written in the early fifties. Despite the implicit sacrifice to male creativity in H.D.'s description of this poem as 'my own *Cantos*' (ET 32), it does attempt to provide some explanation of writing and thought other than the male-centred paradigm.

Helen in Egypt marks a watershed in H.D.'s work. It can be viewed as an attempt to revise or work through the myths and Hellenic concerns of her earlier writing which could be epitomised neatly by simply the titles of some of the early poems: 'The Cliff Temple', 'Sea Gods', 'Acon', 'Hermes of the Ways' and so on. Her versions of Ion, Iphigenia, Hecuba similarly pin-point that concern which cannot be divorced from her fascination with Hellas, with Greece as her symbolic mother-land. But by displacing *Helen in Egypt*, by sending Helen to Egypt that is, H.D. immediately opens up a new space in which to work. The removal allows, in the opening section, 'Palinode', the question of personal identity in relation to the mother to arise. In an earlier prose text, the unpublished 'Notes on Thought and Vision', and also in Advent, what she has described as her 'prenatal fantasy' (a longing for the mother's protective in-difference or for the time before the inscription of the letter) is regarded as disruptive of identity and everyday consciousness — that consciousness being in some sense disruptive because it is 'abnormal', characterised by the 'jelly-fish experience of double-ego' (TF 116) and akin to seeing the world through 'two convex lenses that I called bell-jars' (TF 118). It leads, in other words, to the experience of 'oneness lost, madness' (T 41) which marks the 'Dream Vision' (T 18) of *Trilogy*'s most painful moments — precisely the experiences that precipitated her analysis with Freud.

But *Helen in Egypt* attempts to recuperate that loss of identity in giving an answer to the question 'Helen? who is she?' (HE 37). The presence of Helen in Egypt is specifically to re-order that problem of identity in a new place as Helen

> invokes (as any perceptive visitor to Egypt must always do) the symbol or the 'letter' that represents or recalls the protective mother-goddess. This is no death-symbol, but a life-symbol, it is Isis or her Greek counterpart, Thetis, the mother of Achilles. (HE 13)

H.D.'s own identification with Isis, the mother-wife eternally seeking the son-lover who has disappeared and been dismembered, is emblemised in the figure of this goddess who, like Hilda Doolittle herself parading the siglum H.D., wears the hieroglyph of her name above her head. In that identification is included the mystery of desire in that Helen's lover, Achilles, is the son of Isis' Hellenic counterpart Thetis. By accepting the significance of the letter, the 'living hieroglyph' (HE 23), Helen provokes Achilles' anger and fear and 'became what his accusation made me, Isis' so that *'She (Helen) herself is the writing'* (HE 23).

That writing, 'the indecipherable script' (HE 86), is the mark of female desire and is turned against the men who 'fought, forgetting women' (HE 4). The mode of that language is a stance against the 'purely masculine iron-ring' of warriors of which Achilles is a part. When Achilles is killed by the dart of Eris, whom H.D. transforms into Eros so that he is effectively killed by love or desire, 'the Walls fall' (HE 55), and masculine activity is curtailed. But, resurrected in Egypt, Achilles tries to re-assume the culturally ordered masculine tasks, wanting to 'work to reclaim the coast/with the Pharos, the light-house' (HE 63). Against the rigidity of such masculine structures and pursuits that are bathed in the light of phallic control, Helen is concerned 'to establish or re-establish the ancient Mysteries' or, in other terms, to accept the letter's continual veering towards a semiotic traversal of the structures of male identity and power. This movement of 'a hieroglyph, repeated endlessly' (HE 20) is specifically metonymic, a writing which is, in answer to 'the eternal why of the Sphinx' (HE 93), expansive like 'the spread of wings' (HE 24) or what has been suggested in *Trilogy*, 'a most beautiful fragrance of all flowering things together' (T 172).

As I have said, there is something disturbing finally about H.D.'s

embracing of the metonymic course. It is not simply that it is endowed
with a sort of mystical status, or that it is supposedly the transcendent
condition of woman's desire in language; both those objections could
be raised against other and later feminist texts, such as Laura Mulvey's
film *Riddles of the Sphinx*. That film helps to clarify the position of
H.D.'s symbolical and mystical language by insisting on the unknown
nature of the 'enigmatic script [that] reminds her of a forgotten history
and the power of a different language',[18] and of the necessity of that
mystery's exploration as a resistance to patriarchal language. What the
objection to H.D.'s work must usually be is its view of that mystery as
an ultimately theological one, god-given. Even as Helen becomes 'the
writing, the script,/the thousand-petalled lily' it is in recognition of
belonging in the end to Zeus or Amen, those imperial gods: it is the
'Amen-script' (HE 21).

Here of course another part of the Isis myth is relevant. One of the
favourite books on H.D.'s shelves was M.A. Murray's *Ancient Egyptian
Legends*. In that book we are told the story of how Isis, resentful of
the supreme power of Ra, causes him to be afflicted by a poison that
she alone can counteract: she refuses to act, however, until Ra's power
has been transmitted to her in the form of his unutterable, unknowable name which now passes from his breast to hers. That transmittal
of the ultimate mystery from the god-father is what H.D. sought from
Freud and had been led to expect from her communion with Pound.
Indeed, in *Tribute to Freud* there is the sense that the transmittal leads
to the final feminine victory, to empowered femininity, the where-
withal being precisely in Sigmund Freud's words, in his victorious (Sieg)
mouth (Mund) (TF 105).

This unfortunate tendency is developed somewhat in the second part
of *Helen in Egypt*. Here, there is a further topical remove – this time
from Egypt to Leuke, the white island. Leuke is the place of the dead
and so the removal there allows the reappearance into Helen's sight of
other important figures from her past: Paris, her former lover; Theseus,
who had abducted her when she was young but who now appears as a
sage and protective father; and Euphorion, Helen's aptly named son by
Achilles. With the introduction of these figures, lover, father and son,
the question of desire becomes of primary importance.

Paris is immediately present as 'the so far suppressed memory and
unspoken name'. He represents Helen's 'first rebellion' from the protective influence of the mother and he is at the same time the archetype of
the lost lover and object of female questing. But Helen learns from
Theseus, the now all-seeing grandfather, to view Paris as simply a cipher

in the recognition of the endless renewal of desire: Theseus has told Helen of the continual re-weaving of the metonymic thread of desire, the continual rearticulation of the same stories in the unconscious. It is interesting to note that Theseus was apparently intended to represent Freud himself, according to Norman Holmes Pearson; and also that H.D.'s close friend and lover, Bryher, was coincidentally taught how to read hieroglyphs when she was a child by an unnamed Austrian archaeologist.[19]

That insight offered by Theseus/Freud into the nature of desire, and the metaphor for archaeological excavation that arises from the Bryher connection, are both central to H.D.'s work and are embedded in the project of her novel *Palimpsest*. That book inscribes three versions of the female quest for identity in different times and places: Rome in the first century BC, London during and after the Great War, and Egypt in the twenties. The three sections do not replace each other but are all to be read as it were simultaneously, as different attempts at the retrieval or discovery of an identity, or what Joseph Riddel calls 'the writing signature'.[20] The Roman episode ends with the poetess Hipparchia finding 'the authentic metre' for her versions of the Greek classics; the London section sees Raymonde Ransome similarly achieving a poem by donning 'the helmet of Ray Bart', a masculine *nom de plume*; the Egyptian section is specifically set in 'Excavator's Egypt', the land of hieroglyphs, with the narrator, another Helen, trying to 'dive deep, deep, courageously down into some unexploited region of the consciousness . . . and bring triumphant to the surface some treasure, buried, lost, forgotten'.

There, within the metaphor of the palimpsestic text, all the main themes of H.D.'s exploration of her unconscious are inscribed. It is exactly the overlaying of the three stories, and their multiple resonances with and among themselves and the rest of H.D.'s writing, that vindicate the description of the work as a palimpsest. It is a palimpsest that perhaps is best described by reference to Freud's mystic writing-pad whereon the traces of all previous writing can still be read:

The unconscious is not the message itself, not even the strange or coded message one strives to read on a palimpsest or an old parchment: it is another text written underneath and which must be read by illuminating it from behind or with the help of a developer.[21]

Theseus, the god-father, is that illumination. It is he who enables

Helen to remember the parts of her past that have to be continually re-articulated in the unconscious. He is a central presence to the whole of *Helen in Egypt* (as Freud is to the whole of H.D.'s writing) in so far as he provides the light by which Helen can come to terms with the course of the letter and the fact that 'There is always another and another and another' (HE 167), or that the letter is continually re-presented to the unconscious, demanding articulation. The most useful truth that this realisation leads to is her role, opposed to the Poundian Achilles who 'measured the stars' (HE 205): she is to be the writing by which the situations of her past life are reworked. Helen uses Theseus/Freud's lesson to discover her part in a sort of transmuted Oedipal situation where her previous lover, Paris, is metamorphosed into her son, Euphorion. In a version of the *fort/da* game, rearticulated, 'I lost the lover, Paris/but to find the Son' (HE 155). Just as the child that Freud observed had to enact in his game the departure of his mother in order to achieve the hallucinated satisfaction of her return, so Helen plays with the desire for her deserting lover only to achieve joyful satisfaction in the appearance of Euphorion. Paris is further qualified to act in this drama since he assists in the following equation:

And Eris is this fire-brand (that killed Achilles),
Paris, and Eros is again, the unconquerable child. (HE 184)

Paris can thus take his symbolic place in the Oedipal drama as the emblem of the desire of Helen, his 'mother', and can kill his 'father', Achilles: 'The slayer becomes the son of the slain' (HE 184). This 'fire-brand' reappears in *End to Torment* as the hallucinated son of H.D. and Pound, the 'Wunderkind' mentioned earlier, who is the symbol, as it were, of the deserting lover's reconstituted body.

In this sense, *Helen in Egypt* becomes a celebration of motherhood. It can be seen as the long-delayed mark of a certain coming to terms with the 'jelly-fish experience of double-ego'. Signally enough, H.D. tells us that it was 'before the birth of my child that the jelly-fish consciousness seemed to come definitely into the field or realm of the intellect or brain' or to be circumscribed by the 'iron ring' of patriarchal authority and activity. It is only after the birth of the child, Perdita, that this oceanic feeling can be 'centered in the love-region of the body, or placed like a foetus in the body'. After the experience of motherhood women can come to attain a 'vision of the womb, or love-vision'.[22] It is in the third section of *Helen in Egypt*, 'Eidolon', that the lessons of these explorations are applied. Whereas in the first two sections Helen had been removed from her own mother-land to the Utopia of Egypt and Leuke, in the third section, having been through 'the dream, delirium, trance, ecstacy' of excavation and exploration, the question is 'Where is she now?' (HE 222). The answer appears that 'This is the waking-dream or day-dream', or a version of the real where the lessons of the dream are applied to a waking state.

What essentially Helen has learned from her questioning and questing is that it is the mother Isis' hieroglyph, her writing, which at once can speak against the wordly activity of the male and reveal the presence of the all-powerful transcendent force. What has to be accom-plished is the transfer of that knowledge to the male-lover so that male and female can join together in the world of 'a rhythm as yet unheard' (HE 229), outside of the legislative world of 'Apollo's snare'. Achilles must join Helen in her role as reader of the mysteries and become himself the 'royal sacred High Priest of love-rites' (HE 210). The renunciation of his former world of war and adventuring must be effected by allowing him to discover the secret recognition of the god-mother. He must return his attention to the writing of Isis in her transposed figure as Thetis, his own mother. Thetis is a marine divinity and so Achilles has to succumb to 'his mother, the sea-enchantment' (HE 272) in an experience that could be the equiva-lent of H.D.'s 'jelly-fish experience' or her 'pre-natal fantasy'. Through the plunging of Achilles into this recognition which will allow him access to the deathly peace of the end of desire should come the 'one moment' (HE 303) that is the goal of all H.D.'s writing. He must take cognisance of the name, the letter that 'Thetis . . . would brand on his forehead'.

It is in this equivalent recognition that an equality of male and female fears and desires could be set up. Helen asks:

Did he fear her [Thetis] more
than I could ever fear
the pad of paws on the sand,

the glare of eyes in the fire,
the lion or the crouching panther? (HE 271)

In these lines is inscribed H.D.'s own fear of the masculine gaze of phallic power, the 'X-Ray' of Ezra who is also known in *End to Torment* as a predatory cat. The equivalent male fears are of motherhood as it resists the activity of patriarchy, as it questions it in the manner of the Sphinx. Achilles, standing perhaps for the conscious mind, has to be made aware of the unconscious as it is situated in relation to the mother, the mother's letter branded on his skin. Whilst this would seem to be what we might call an essentialist feminism — virtually identifying woman with the unconscious much as Lacan does in *Encore* — it does have the strategic value of enforcing a review of what the unconscious should appear like to a man caught in the trammels of the Apollonian world of social organisation.[23]

It is in this recommendation and its working-out that *Helen in Egypt* appears to me to be pre-eminent among H.D.'s poems. And for all its simplistic equating of the unconscious with woman's 'natural' state, it also contains an implicit stance against the writing of Pound and its disavowal of the letter — a disavowal which is almost a driving principle in the *Cantos*. Helen stands for another kind of writing presided over by the images of weaving and enigmatic script, images which relate to the existence of the notion of the rebus in the unconscious. H.D.'s writing is able to suggest the possibility of its own metonymic strategies as a sort of specifically feminine language: when we are told that 'Helen is the Greek drama . . . she herself is the writing' (HE 91) it is so that we may see the questions raised in H.D.'s work as questions of female identity and of the drama of feminine accession to a symbolic realm which is structured by patriarchal principles. The deficiency, as I see it, of H.D.'s work lies in its ultimate resolution of this new separateness, the multiple hieroglyphs of the woven thread, into the word of an all-powerful god-father.

The Amen that underlies the 'Dream Vision', whatever the extent to which he can be said to be reached by strategies of feminist exploration, is specifically male. As a ratificatory signature to the text, as the amen of imprecation or of the profession of faith, Amen dissipates some of the force of H.D.'s enquiry. To see H.D. as a specifically feminist writer must, then, be to ignore the problem of that faith in a final resolutory figure. The writing finally gives its support to a traditional female/male position. An analysis by Martine Liebovici of 'La Position Féminine dans la Bible'[24] explicates that whole question of female accession to language by noting that speech is not available to Adam in *Genesis* except after he has seen the woman, different (and) from himself, who represents to him a loss. Without woman, man would not have been able to differentiate himself and so not have been able to attain the sort of language that we have; that is, a language instituted by the fact of somatic and thus symbolic differentiation. He would have been unable then to take up his place as the image of God — and what, in H.D.'s work, is the male if not an image of a god?

So, the reliance of patriarchal language upon seeing the woman as difference is finally vindicated by H.D. Still the question remains as to how women can speak and what language can it be? Laura Mulvey's film asks the same question and answers it in a way which, however tentative, points to some of the more remarkable passages in H.D.'s work:

> What could the pattern of the embroidery be? She imagined an intricate web of curved forms, intertwined knots, like the tendrils and fronds in the marsh where, according to Bachofen, the first matriarchy rose, or the curls of pubic hair from which, according to Freud, women wove the first veil.[25]

It is to this reticular structure of language and history, the psychic and the social, that *Trilogy* refers as the charge of the writer:

> we are the keepers of the secret,
> the carriers, the spinners
>
> of the rare intangible thread
> that binds all humanity
>
> to ancient wisdom,
> to antiquity (T 24)

It is probably hardly worth pointing out that this is a totally different conception of the binding thread that weaves things together from Pound's.

The project of that sort of writing for those divorced from 'the habits of the lordly fixed ones' (T 45) is to follow 'the peculiar orbit' of the unconscious in recognition of Freud's view of that site of meaning and the subject's construction. It is a writing which provokes the sort of transgression of established social values that is epitomised by the picture of Mary Magdalene 'seated on the floor', paying no attention to the strictures of society around her, deftly un-weaving

the long, carefully-braided tresses
of her extraordinary hair (T 141)

The fruit of that perverse unweaving is exactly in the sort of passage as
the following, where Mary Magdalene's name is metonymically
explored:

I am Mary, she said, of a tower-town,
or once it must have been towered

for Magdala is a tower;
Magdala stands on the shore;

I am Mary, she said, of Magdala,
I am Mary, a great tower;

through my will and my power,
Mary shall be myrrh;

I am Mary — O, there are Marys a-plenty,
(though I am Mara, bitter) I shall be Mary-myrrh;

I am that myrrh-tree of the gentiles,
the heathen: there are idolaters,

even in Phrygia and Cappadocia,
who kneel before mutilated images

and burn incense to the Mother of Mutilations,
to Attis-Adonis-Tammuz and his mother who was myrrh;

she was a stricken woman,
having borne a son in unhallowed fashion;

she wept bitterly till some heathen god
changed her to a myrrh-tree;

I am Mary, I will weep bitterly,
bitterly ... bitterly. (T 135)

Mary's name includes the notion of a tower in competition with Achilles' Pharos; it also relates to the fragrance of Myrrh which is doubly inscribed in that it is an epitome of 'a most beautiful fragrance/ as of all things flowering at once' (T 172) but also a tribute to Christ, and so registers what I have been describing as the tensions of H.D.'s entire output. But myrrh also takes on different meanings: it is the incense burnt in honour of Cybele, the castrated mother-goddess who in fact was changed into a myrrh bush, weeping in a bitter (mara) way; Myrrha, of course, was also the mother of Adonis, a sort of 'Wunder-kind'. This passage literally unveils the traditionally covered face of that mother-goddess, flaunting the conventions of religious law and exposing her powers of transformation and generation, in the language that arises from the root of her name.

One critic, a male, has said that this passage 'resembling a game of phonics controlled only by the demands of the theme, is more likely to strike the reader as silly than stimulating',[26] but his objections have already been forestalled by H.D.'s ironic recognition through the eyes of Kaspar (a metamorphosis of the Mage who had carried myrrh to Christ's nativity) that

> it was hardly decent of her to stand there,
> unveiled, in the house of a stranger. (T 134)

Quinn's remarks are simply a mark of the inability of traditional criticism — itself a staunchly patriarchal institution — to come to terms with what Helen has been trying to teach Achilles. It is interesting, too, to see another representative of the institution of literature attempt to defend the modes of masculine demeanour against whatever threat H.D. poses: I am referring to D.H. Lawrence. His story, *The Man Who Died*, apparently uses H.D. as the model for the priestess of Isis to whom the resurrected Christ goes for refreshment.[27] She is one of the 'rare women who wait for the re-born man'[28] in all due humility and patience. But as she anoints his wounds 'the vitals of the man howled in pain'[29] and he deserts her. The pain that the priestess/H.D. causes him is specifically linguistic: 'The word is but the midge that bites at evening. Man is tormented with words like midges, and they follow him right into the tomb.'[30] As the *word* that H.D.'s writing offers causes the revival of the anguish of desire, the disruption of the subject's certainty, the man leaves.

The unveiling of the letter of the great-mother in all her materiality is effected in following the metonymic course through that word, doing away with the repressive metaphors that would halt the flow of desire in the realm of paternal influence. It is exactly as a dismissal of the objections by the male-critics that this sort of writing functions. He who is so dismissive of the practice is in fact outraged by its excessiveness, or by the revelation of female desire 'in so far as it is *en plus*, something more'[31] than patriarchy can legislate for; in that situation the representatives of patriarchy opt for demeaning the woman by whatever abusive means they can — Pound, as we have seen, is especially adept. But it is precisely in that 'something more' that H.D. can suggest, to borrow Stephen Heath's formulation, 'the possibility of a specifically feminine practice of writing in language, where writing is understood in a modern perspective as an activity of transgression breaking with the fixed positions of language, opening out a moving tissue of meanings'.[32]

H.D.'s last written work has been collected under the title of *Hermetic Definition*: in that collection we find 'Hermetic Definition' itself, 'Sagesse', and a sort of coda to *Helen in Egypt* called 'Winter Love'. All the tendencies that I have tried to point out in H.D.'s work are reinscribed in these three poems. They all build on the sort of polarities that are familiar, in a movement that is most explicit in the cold/warmth and night/day antinomies that form the central core to 'Sagesse', towards a recognition of the ruling powers that 'share [the] name, *Soleil*' (the sun/son) (HD 84), but still passing through the agency of the 'Grande Mer, patron and protectress' (HD 73). In these poems there is a sort of Joycean 'echo of the sea, our secret/and our simple mystery, Grande Mer' (or *grande-mère*) (HD 75).

In these poems there is the recognition of the wounded mother, the Cybele-figure, the *grande-mère* who stands behind the Oedipal structure in the locus of woman's access to the symbolic in the 'diastole, systole' (HD 65) movement of the unconscious. It is the 'old grandam' who embodies in 'Winter Love' the law of 'repetition, repetition' (HD 90), the unendingness of desire and its metonymic displacements. Always

> there is something left over,
> the first unsatisfied desire. (HD 91)

'Winter Love', written after what we might call the exorcism of Pound in *End to Torment*, embraces the 'thick skein/woven on tangled memory and desire' (HD 103) and achieves a certain satisfaction through the writing of the poem itself. That new equilibrium is mapped on to a set of strophes and antistrophes, the diastolic and systolic beat of the unconscious's reality. The first strophe is negative, bemoaning 'the breach in the Wall/that sears like a gaping wound' (HD 93), but the antistrophe is creative, recommending the

> re-weaving with threads of gold,
> cyclamen, purple and blue,
> the pattern, the history,
> the legend. (HD 94)

And when the second strophe then questions 'What song is left to sing' (HD 95) the new antistrophe reinstates the possibility of hope with its

> Heed not the dissonance,
> Heed not the hiss of Death
> . . .
> Recall first love and last. (HD 96)

That past and present love is, of course, embodied in the male-child Euphorion, 'Esperance, the infinite bliss/living in the hope of something that will be,/the past made perfect' (HD 112).

It is not until 'Hermetic Definition' that the equation that has been suggested throughout H.D.'s work, hovering over it, is actually made explicit: the 'Wunderkind' is writing itself, the very poem. Out of the course of her love for Lionel Durand, the frustrated story of which emotion 'Hermetic Definition' describes, comes the poem itself nine months later: 'It was April that we met' (HD 49) and a little over nine months 'to the day . . . you were born' (HD 48). This is the final manifestation of the reconstituting of the lost lover's body in the defiles of the signifier. It is a linguistic hallucination for the satisfaction of H.D.'s desire, or rather the *literal* term to Freud's 'symbolic equation — from the penis to the baby'.

In an article about *Hermetic Definition*, Vincent Quinn points out that in the completion of the poem 'the physical reality of the young man (Durand), which has hung in unsteady balance with his symbolic (Osiris) role, now almost completely disappears'.[33] Indeed, the final section of 'Hermetic Definition' demands this of the lover:

> Now you are born
> and it's all over,
> will you leave me alone? (HD 55)

Once the son-poem is accomplished the male-lover can disappear: here again we can refer to the *fort/da* game where the presence that is constructed by the throwing away of the object does away with the anxiety of absence in a 'catastrophic moment of entrance into an universal order'. As Martin Thom explains, this moment of cultural (linguistic) achievement 'entails the installation of a repetition compulsion' – familiar to H.D. – promising 'an ideal *jouissance* in a future time'.[34] Out of that achievement H.D. can come to

know adequately

the reddest rose,
the unalterable law . . .
Night brings the Day (HD 55)

and so achieve the equilibrium she has been seeking.

Just as Durand's presence can be dispensed with after the writing itself has taken its course, after its separation from the mother's body (a separation which bespeaks the renewal of desire), so Ezra Pound can be dispensed with after the writing across his body that *End to Torment* constitutes. The final sections of that latter book are marked by Pound's disappearance to Italy with the letter that really stays with H.D. and by a symbolic rose. An instance of the necessity and importance of that final disappearance is in H.D.'s comment while writing the memoir that 'I have only lately dared to try to read the *Cantos*'(ET 30), overcoming her feeling, expressed in an earlier letter to Viola Jordan, that 'I found the *Cantos* heartbreaking.'[35] It is not long after the completion of *End to Torment* that 'Hermetic Definition', with its final resolutory metaphor, was written. The title, as I pointed out before, restores to the siglum H.D. what Pound had removed. This can be seen as the long-delayed discovery of the writing signature that Riddel talks of, and it corroborates H.D.'s new-found determination that 'I can't think that I *must* be Pound-Eliot' in writing.[36]

In other words, there is no longer a competition with male creativity. Through the paths of her metonymic writing and the excesses of that mode which upset the critics so much, H.D. appears to find the force which she predicted would be 'resurrected or re-born once Ezra is free' (ET 37), free not only from St Elizabeths but from the constricting fears and black-outs that H.D. had established for herself in relation to his image. By writing itself she has removed the threat of his actual and metaphorical gaze. When she speaks in *End to Torment* of the 'terror one cannot speak of' (ET 7) that strikes her in contempating the idea of having another X-ray performed on her broken limbs, she was succumbing to Pound's phallic power — not only is the X-ray that gaze which is capable of pointing out any supposed defects of her anatomy but it is the young Pound's creative signature. But H.D. has written herself out of the lines of that gaze by the end of her life, utilising writing itself, her own unconscious, a retreat to the involucrum: 'we must present another self, a shell' (HD 68), the place of the unconscious in its resistance to patriarchal structures and Pound in particular.

7 Z-SITED: ZUKOFSKY'S A

Louis Zukofsky's poetry has long been situated in a sort of penumbra which only now is beginning to recede. For many years critical attention to Zukofsky's work has been thin on the ground, although at the same time many modern and contemporary poets have been profoundly interested in his work.[1] In so far as he has been admitted at all into the modern canon he seems to be considered largely as a disciple of Pound's (a view which is implicitly, though not unquestioningly, corroborated by his posthumous adoption by the journal of Pound studies, *Paideuma*).[2] It is clearly true that Zukofsky and Pound shared a great deal, not least a friendship that lasted over forty years. Yet the reader approaching *A* for the first time will not, I think, be easily able to reconcile the modes of Zukofsky's writing to those of Pound: I want to try to point out here that, even if Zukofsky's work begins its course under the aegis and tutelage of Pound's work, it finishes as an exemplary counterbalance to the older poet and finally represents a sustained and important attempt to write a way out of his shadow.

In 1932 the young Zukofsky edited the now celebrated *An 'Objectivists' Anthology*. That book was primarily an attempt to float the work of young American poets such as Williams, Oppen, Rakosi, Reznikoff and Zukofsky himself. But it also had the shadow of Pound all across it, not least in its making room for some pages of Pound's worst doggerel. Pound's piece is in a familiar style, couched in his imitative 'yiddisher voice' and satirising the influence of the Jews on American society: supposedly, 'Calvin Coolidge dh'pvwezident' is one receptor of that influence, and it is suggested that 'Bloomsburee/Where the soup tastes like last night's gravee' would be an appropriate burial place for him and other perverters of civilisation.[3] Apparently, this verse comes from Pound's correspondence with Zukofsky and its inclusion in the anthology, alongside the first sections of *A* and much other serious work (notably Williams' *Spring and All*), has the effect of demeaning the younger writers' work. However, it could well be that the piece was included as a salutary indication of Pound's propensity to stray from what Zukofsky's dedicatory preface to him describes as 'himself masterly engaging/an inference of musical self-criticism'.[4] Indeed, there is in that very dedication an overt, if restrained, criticism of Pound. The anthology is given to him despite 'the fact that his epic discourse always his own choice of matter causes him in his *Cantos* to write syntactically almost no two lines the consecutiveness of which includes less than two phrases'. That criticism, underneath Zukofsky's careful convolutions of phrase, is content with a glance at Pound's choice of subject matter for his poem and gives way, in any case, to the judgement that Pound 'is still for the poets of our time the most important'. And yet there is a definite unease, nestling beneath Zukofsky's words, towards the grand Poundian manner; and I think that the inclusion of the Poundian doggerel is possibly a signal to the reader as to what faults Pound can be accused of.

A further mark of such a tension can perhaps be glimpsed in the epigraph that immediately follows the preface. This is a quotation from René Taupin which recommends that poets 'find again the essential distinction of the epic, which is neither love nor hate but the restitution of these sentiments to a chain of facts which exist and the existence of which confers upon them the marvellous'.[5] This can be read as a gentle picking of a quarrel with Pound's increasing desire to move the *Cantos* into the strictly polarised view of social relations that we are familiar with, at the expense of the specificity of poetic discourse and its procedures. This is really the only strain of criticism that Zukofsky ever allowed himself to indulge in with regard to Pound whom he always revered as a master poet, a poetic father,[6] but whose substantive concerns he never appreciated. The role of those concerns in the making of poetry was indeed the cause of some coolness in relations between the two men in 1933 when Pound, piqued by Zukofsky's rejection of some of his economic ideas, threatened to exclude Zukofsky from his next anthology which would consist of work by poets who were aware of the import of economics to their poetic discourse.[7] Of course, a reading of *A* shows clearly that Zukofsky was also similarly aware of the importance of economic determination — Veblen and Marx both appear frequently in the early parts of *A* and in Zukofsky's shorter poems. But for Zukofsky the problem was never as simple as it seemed to be for Pound: he was always concerned to see that Pound's writing showed precisely the imbalance that I have pointed out — that, in other words, the poet's concern with substance had distracted him from the qualities and operations of language itself.

After Pound's arrest and trial for treason after World War II Zukofsky writes of his difficulties with Pound's obsessions:

When he was here in 1939, I told him that I did not doubt his integrity had decided his political action, but I pointed to his head, indicating that something had gone wrong. When he asked me if it was possible to educate certain politicians, I retorted, Whatever you don't know, Ezra, you ought to know *voices.*[8]

Zukofsky's point is clearly that the poet's ear for language, once unparalleled in finesse, had been seduced by the sirens of the fixed world of politics. Pound's reply to that criticism can be seen later in a poem called 'Old Zuk', published in 1959:

> This is the grave of old Zuk
> who wasn't really a crook
> but who died of persistence
> in that non-existence
>   which consists in refusing to LOOK.[9]

Here, once more, re-emerges the opposition between language and sight, with Zukofsky set firmly on the side of the voice against the presumptions of the power of the eye. For Pound it would be self-evidently true that anyone who bothered to look would see the same things as he himself saw, so anyone who appears not to agree with him obviously cannot be looking very hard.

It is within the context of this opposition that Zukofsky writes *A*. The early parts of that poem have Pound very much in mind and, indeed, they have certain similarities to the epic that Pound was writing that cannot be overlooked. Kenneth Cox has pointed out the Zukofskian appropriation of Pound's conversational language, the use of anecdote and extended quotation and the note of protest that runs through many of the pieces is *A 1-12*.[10] The gathering together of materials of many different provenances to form an organic flowing structure is, though, the primary device that Zukofsky took from Pound, to the extent that this familiar Poundian technique appears undiluted — as in *A-8* for example. That movement contains the most Poundian of all Zukofsky's writing as it attacks the way in which labour is 'Betrayed and sold' (A 47), and echoes Pound's epistemology in passages such as this:

> The facts are not strange to each other.
> When they drive, your choice
> Cannot but be guided by simplicity.

> Not enough to reject the falsely related,
> The mirrors of the facts must not be dissimulated. (A 47/8)

Indeed, at the time of writing this Zukofsky was concerned to remark his similarities with Pound. In a letter to Pound in April 1935 he not only suggests that his writing deals with much the same substantive concerns as Pound's 'Eleven New Cantos' which had just appeared, but he even adopts Pound's own epistolatory style to do so: 'So-o-o unless Dame Philoserfy misleads me, we must have both gathered our matter by perception.'[11]

Zukofsky's attempts to align his own work with Pound's, his effort at emulating the master, are always accompanied by something ambivalent, some concern which is in excess of Pound's own. It is this something more which causes the debate between the two men. Zukofsky cannot live up to Pound's demands in being economics conscious — apparently — and to that extent fails the legislative demands of his poetic father. Yet Zukofsky can berate Pound because 'you no longer bother to weigh each word you handle, translate etc. The damn foreigner you say I am has more respect for English than you have.'[12] It is precisely the attention to the materiality of the words which make up poems that is always the mark of difference between Pound and Zukofsky and which is at the root of Zukofsky's poetics as it revises Pound's. Even within these early parts of *A* which live in Pound's shadow, there is a sense that the writing is formulating itself into a criticism of Pound's vehicular use of poetry whereby the weight of those concerns of Pound's is subverted by the poem itself. There is always a continued discussion within *A 1-12* about the relation of song to those concerns which seems to suggest that the poem's very process should constitute a casting-off of the division between the problems of the economic real and poetry's relation to that real. A dialectic is established between the two sides of the division which can be solved by the actual utterance as it takes its form within 'contemporary and historical particulars'.[13] Early on, in 'A-2', Zukofsky had rejected the notion of a solipsistic music which would, in a self-congratulatory manner, put aside contemporary problems; and so some notion of what the song represents in the passes of that dialectic had to be established.

Zukofsky's attempt to fulfil that task works by a definite but simple musical analogy. A writing that deals with the particulars of the modern world must present, out of the *divisions* that the world presents, a model of harmony. I take it that *A 1-12* is the preparatory work towards that end, vindicating in *A 13-21* what might appear as the idealist strain of the proposed solution by presenting the song itself, an exemplum of the required harmony. The project has its announcement in 'A-6':

> O heart,
>   how
>   the
>   blood
> And the measures (travel outward)
> Should travel together. (A 21)

The 'travel outward' into the world must be reconciled with the individual body, so that the body as it exists in the world of particulars can take its measure from the form of the language that it has available, its measures: the poem *A* is an attempt to offer 'The common air' (A 26), a new availability in language which can even, in Zukofsky's extreme suggestion, sustain that body through the exigencies of the world in which it is doomed to exploitation by the structuring powers.

Although Zukofsky declined to be identified as a Communist — perhaps for the sake of a certain ease of passage through the anti-Communist hysterics of mid-century America[14] — there can be no doubt that his sympathies lie in the opposite path to Pound's. Whereas Pound appeals to the teleology of natural process and to the identificatory lures that underpin Fascism, Zukofsky's thrust is toward the Marxist theory of labour, a hatred of corporatism and a lack of confidence in the notion of the great hero-leader. His concern is, in a conventionally American way, with the individual and with the ideological problems that arise from seeing 'Labor as creator, Labor as creature' (A 43). But against that conventional outlook is the recognition that, in the very formula I just quoted, the individual is irremediably split: countering Pound's corporate notion of the *individual* Zukofsky might wish to argue with that word's very etymology. The split in the subject's role is reflected obliquely in Zukofsky's ambivalence towards his own role as labourer, as writer. Seeing himself labouring, concerned with the material of language, he is caught between the status as creature, a demeaned and exploited (indeed, sometimes ignored) labourer, and that of the creator attempting to establish the unexploitable value and dignity of his work. That double-bind is conveniently summed up in Zukofsky's laconic quotation in his *Autobiography* from e.e. cummings:

> As for subsistence I can only quote with
> affection e.e. cummings: 'no thanks.'[15]

The poet as creature is given no thanks, and to the system in which he, like any other labourer, is fixed he says, 'no thanks.'

It is in this attitude, a polite refusal of the array of positions which inform political life, that Zukofsky approaches the stance of James Joyce who, as I have said, presented his writing as a mode of exit from the fixed systems of exchange which political activism necessarily has a part in. Of course, any writer who would adopt this strategy must produce the model of discourse which, like *Finnegans Wake*, has the claimed subversive effect, or else he must be accused of indifference and individualism. *A* and Zukofsky have, of course, been accused of as much, or worse. Eric Motrram's essay '1924-1951: Politics and Form in Zukofsky' is devoted to showing how *A* specifically rests in 'hand-wringing liberalism' and even attempts 'to re-establish confidence in American mores rather than changing them radically from the base up'.[16] Another critic, Michael Heller, is at pains to remind us of the 'profoundly conservative effort' that Zukofsky's work makes and that 'its value for the poet lies precisely in its conservatory nature'.[17] It should be said that both these critics are directing their remarks at the early sections of *A*, not at the work which I take to be the later attainment of Zukofsky's goal, but I assume the authors would still wish to extend their comments to the rest of *A* with its ostensible remove to the domain of the bourgeois family – to Zukofsky's wife, Celia, and son, Paul. However, it is on the base of that removal, Zukofsky's version of the retreat into the involucrum, that I intend to build my case for his writing which I regard as an example of how the careful attention to linguistic strategies can offer ways to political change that are the ways, precisely, of the outsider, the man who says 'no thanks' to the whole system of which the oscillations of factional political argument are part.

A 1-12 progresses in a series of antiphonal voices: 'one song of many voices' (A 18), 'The song out of the voices' (A 8). One critic has seen the movements as an alternation of subjective and objective utterance, the odd-numbered sections being subjective and the even objective.[18] While I would not wish to embrace that description or its vocabulary, it is true to say that the even-numbered sections are in a way *responses* to the others: and it is in the former that Zukofsky explicates his poetic and political ideas, whereas in the latter it is the performance and utterance of the song itself that are highlighted.

That loose structural principle is reflected in the first two movements of the poem. 'A-1', written at the time of the Depression, offers a picture of the poet ready to, as it were, sing his way out of the exigencies of the times: the music of Bach's Matthew Passion at a Carnegie Hall concert has an uplifting effect which promises the subject the 'flower-cell, liveforever, before the eyes, perfecting' (A 4), the ideal clear music which can ignore the real. But even immediately after the concert that real intrudes by the agency of 'the voices of those who had been at the concert' (A 2), and by talk overheard about 'the Pennsylvania miners . . . again on the lockout' (A 3). The perfection of the music is seductive, but it is 'as beyond effort − /Music leaving no traces,/Not dying, and leaving no traces' (A 4); its spell is broken by the real world.

If 'A-1' seems to resent that intrusion of the world on to its music, then it is immediately answered by 'A-2' where, in dialogue with someone called Kay, the poet, 'defending "A-1" against its first critic',[19] explains what his project will be. He describes a ship of sailors from the Greek epics as they travel their paideuma in a cacophony of noise: 'Laughter . . . Gibes from the low deck . . . scuttling and laughter . . . clatter of waves' (A 6/7). That variegation of sound continues until

> . . . the moon, one afternoon,
> Launches with sea-whorl,
> Opening leaf within leaf floats, green,
> On waves, liveforever . . .
> The music is in the flower. (A 7)

It is that liveforever efflorescence that gives the poet his aim:

> Faces and forms, I would write you down
> In a style of leaves growing. (A 8)

In a sense, this too is Poundian: the dream of a form of perfection which will emerge from the chaotic particulars of the world and human bodies and activities. But whereas in Pound the realisation of that 'forma' is *given*, a metaphysical event of epiphany, what *A* is working towards is a piece of writing, a particular form of language. This will not mark a transcendence of the particulars of the real in an ecstatic vision, but will be something more humble, something caught in language and the real. Zukofsky's 'perfection or focus' is organic, a form arising from language and the body, not something pre-existent, ready to be imposed upon the poem. He is looking for a song which, as a result of the labour done on the matter of language, can enter as sort of corrective into the world of political and social discontent and discord.

It is interesting to note, in this respect, that Zukofsky's poem begins at the time of the Depression and attempts to include and work upon its problems: the Depression is an area of American history that Pound leaves well alone, even though it might have provided him with substantial material about the failure of American capitalism. His unwillingness to deal with those problems is here rectified by Zukofsky, so that *A* is immediately a response to Pound's poem, as well as heir to it; *A* begins speaking in the gaps, as it were, of Pound's discourse.

Zukofsky's poem is also explicitly concerned with the very problem of Pound's epic poem which was never solved: the Poundian paideuma never came to an end and Pound never came home (just as *Paideuma* endlessly circulates around the *Cantos*, hoping for – but never reaching – its exhaustive meaning). Zukofsky's answering song has the home, be it America simply, or 'wherever we put our hats' (A 12), firmly in view. Indeed, to safeguard its completion Zukofsky gave his poem a template, that of the alphabet, beginning with A and ending with his signatory Z. His poem was always 'z-sited. (A 563). He took his template from Chaucer's 'An ABC', which also has only 23 parts[20] (although the complete *A* has twenty-four, the last part being the resolutory music of Celia Zukofsky which signs the statement of deference to music that the whole poem consists in).

It is the inability of the Poundian epic to arrive home, to hang up its hat, that Zukofsky would see as one of its flaws. His own epic, progressing across the dyadic motion I have described, always sees music and song as the metaphor for home. Music, in a sense, *is* the paideuma and it offers the end of the epic not only in that it actually closes the poem, but in that it should always be kept in mind as the poem's purpose: it comes to represent the 'peace between the two contending forces' at the end of the *Odyssey*, and it is also the city that Gilgamesh builds at the end of his story.[21] And music has, of course, its divisions out of which harmony grows. The fact is reflected in the antiphonal structure[22] of two particular parts of *A*, 'A-7' and 'A-9' which are, I take it, the book's first attempts to actually proffer the harmony which

Zukofsky is searching for.

'A-7' is a series of seven sonnets that are spoken and sung altern-
ately in the same way as 'A-1' and 'A–2' answer each other. These
sonnets represent the poet meditating, while 'sat on a stoop', the A-
shaped trestle from which words are hung at the entrance to a street:
' "Street Closed" is what print says on their stomachs' (A 39). The
meditation is as to whether or not the street *is* closed, whether or not
words can find a way through the complexities and obstructions of
modern life. The first voice is a speaking voice that asks 'who will do
it?' (A 39), who will open up the street; this voice remains a questioning, doubting voice which has 'no singing gut' (A 41) and resists the
singing voice's claim that the world can be transformed in words by
purely linguistic attention. But the singing voice wins out: the speaking voice's objections are in the form of a 'But . . .' which the other voice
turns into 'butt', suggesting that the man who is limited to seeing that
the trestles, the horses on which he is sat, 'had no manes', that 'their
wood is dead' and they 'won't pass thru a hoop' (A 40), is really just
sitting on his butt. The singer sees ways of transforming the trestles
into a song which can speak in some sort of enlightenment, and enable
the diggers, the labourers on the enclosed street, to dance and jig,
lightened in their load knowing that their labour need not be exploited.
The importance of 'A-7' is in that battle cry which exists purely by
virtue of the singing voice's transformation in its picture of the real:
the real need not be fixed, language says — and language itself, which
upholds the real, should not be fixed either, or reduced to the commodity of conventional meaning.

It is this performance of encouragement that 'A-9' picks up on.
'A-9' consists of two canzone which have the same rhyme-scheme (that
is, they use the same rhyme words), only the topic of the first is 'things
related as equated values' (A 106) in a theory of labour, while the
second deals with 'values/The measure all use who conceive love' (A
108). The first might be construed as the speaking voice, discussing in
vaguely Marxist terms the appropriation of labour into a system of
values — a system which Zukofsky attacks for its abstracting principles.
It is a system which, by depriving labour of its deeds (cf. A 66) and by
exploiting it so that the goods it produces are unavailable to it, specifically devalues labour. This first canzon is an effort to demonstrate an
opposite principle of undemeaned labour: true labour is put into the
'song's exaction' (A 108). The canzon ends with those words, thus
claiming that the linguistic proprieties that it assumes can force

abstraction to turn from equated
Values to labor we have approximated.

In other words, the actual production of the song by Zukofsky's own labour — the labour which says to and receives from the system 'no thanks' — represents work done from the outside of the demeaning and abstracting system of values which upholds capitalism.

I have suggested before what Pound's position with regard to the system of values that capitalism sustains can tell us about his writing practice. The juridical relations which exist in traditional systems of exchange serve to fix the subject in a given position in order to guarantee the possibility of commodities entering the correct relations with one another, proprietorship being thereby easily recognisable and upheld. Pound's economic theories attempt to tighten that system and its relations in order to attain an unprecedented efficiency in the system. As for writing, so it is for economics. The relation of his writing to that system is that it attempts the fixing of relations between author, text and reader so that the commodity that writing offers — that is, meaning — can be safely and efficiently exchanged. Along the paths of this exchange the materiality of writing is ignored or elided — in any case, devalued — in the name of fixity. For Zukofsky the structure of those relations which Pound is trying to make more fixed is already threatening enough as it deprives labour of its due value, and that means, in the poet's case, the denigration of language. For Zukofsky, then, writing is not to uphold the systems of exchange upon which our society is traditionally based, but to insert into that schema a full regard for the goods created by labour, for the poem as poem.

Zukofsky's effect here can be seen as an insertion into the Marxist analysis of exchange and use values the further complicating factor of language itself. His text jibes well with Barthes' contention that 'Writing is that neutral, composite, oblique space where our subject slips away, the negative where all identity is lost, starting with the very identity of the body writing.'[23] It is perhaps the recognition of those characteristics of writing that prompted a certain revision in the first parts of *A* published in *An 'Objectivists' Anthology*: there Zukofsky's name was inscribed in various modes into the text ('Zukofsky' . . . Zoo-zoo-kaw-kaw-of-the-sky . . . Zoo-kaw-kaw-someone' being good examples since the transformations can indicate an increasing unease with the fact of the name's inscription)[24] but these names do not appear in the book form of *A*. This is a stratagem which begins to act on 'the necessity to substitute language itself for the person who . . . had been supposed to be its owner'.[25]

It is that ownership that Pound adheres to and wishes to guarantee, as it is at the root of the institutionalisation of the author whose work can be viewed as through an understanding of the writing subject's biography and personality. It is, then, not merely modesty but the indication of a serious questioning of that cult that causes Zukofsky to write his autobiography in the form of seventeen of his poems set to music by Celia and interspersed with just five very short paragraphs relating 'the bare facts'.[26] It is, furthermore, no accident that Zukofsky knew and greatly admired the work of Mallarmé, whose celebrated ideal (which gives Barthes his starting point in the essay I have been quoting) was to effect 'la disparition élocutoire du poète'.[27]

Barthes' discussion on the death of the Poundian authorial figure is couched in terms which clearly derive from Lacan. He sees the beginning of writing as the author entering into his own death. The assumption of that death is seen by Lacan as the sacrifice of the subject's homogeneous self to the law of the father, the recognition of lack and division of which Zukofsky's ambivalence to Pound and also the dyadic structure of *A* are both marks. That lack, the 'hole in the real that results from loss [is what] sets the signifier in motion'.[28] A 1-12, in its two-voice structuring, mimes the ambivalence to the father-poet that Zukofsky must go through: forever exasperated by Pound, Zukofsky none the less refuses to attack him publicly, preferring to stress his humanity and to attach to the harmony that could be possible between father and son despite their differences and tensions.[29] This harmony is, of course, the whole aim of *A*, and the relationship between the two poets is transferred to Zukofsky's writing about his own son. The possibility of harmony is the result of the symbolic acceptance of the father which, for Freud, is the result of the successful dissolution of the Oedipus complex. But for Lacan, with his stress on the symbolic functions of all activity, it is in that acceptance, a self-sacrificing one in its recognition of the subject's division, that the metonymic course of desire is set moving: it is the homogeneous subject's death which causes the insertion, into any social analysis, of the subject's consequent mourning − it is here that the death of Pound, the symbolic father, and the death of Zukofsky's real father become important and, indeed, conflated.[30]

Kenneth Cox reports that 'A-12' not only shows that Zukofsky was 'moved to the depths by the death of his father' Reb Pinchos,[31] but that the text where this grief is recorded also contains the 'last relics of the Poundian canon', after which Pound disappears. The two events are linked in that they signal the end of the questioning process of *A 1-12* and open up the vistas of the kind of writing that Zukofsky has been intending, a writing which cannot any longer record the anxiety of division but which accepts it and follows the course of its desire into a writing which no longer has the aim of 'acting directly on reality' but wishes to act 'intransitively . . . finally outside of any function other than the very practice of the symbol itself'.[32] The poem's putting aside of Pound's canon is marked by its using as a structural prop Book XI of the *Odyssey* where Odysseus voyages to Hell to interrogate the spirits, notably that of his mother. It is a voyage into death which takes us to the beginning of Pound's epic where writing should have started. But Pound's poem, beginning with 'And then . . . ', always has a *pretext*, always has something to refer back to – namely the presence of the author as controlling and orchestrating power.

Zukofsky's poem, however, begins with A, the first letter of the alphabet (the 'allaphbed') and so is constrained to start with writing itself, there where the symbolic is immediately cut off from the writer's control. It starts, too, with the body that is writing, or the writing that is body – an equivalence established in 'A-12' with its 'First glyph . . . First body' (A 126), a link which is developed from 'A-7' where 'two legs stand (like) A' (A 39), to 'A-12' where we find 'that broken triangle – standing like you' (A 141). The broken triangle has, of course, its affinities with ALP's 'isocelating biangle', the mark of the unattainable origin of desire.

Zukofsky's suggestion throughout 'A-12' is that it is exactly the poem's articulation, its bodily gestures ('words', after all, 'have knees' (A 18)) which permit the body its lightness and its ability to transcend the deathly, fixed position it finds itself in:

> I think about that in us
> That does not die.
> I grow leaves. (A 146)

The growing of the leaves of the liveforever flower is what *A* is all about. It is the efflorescence of the child from the influence of the father. The process has been ironically commented upon in 'A-4', where the Jewish father is quoted as saying that 'We had a Speech, our children have evolved a jargon' (A 12). Zukofsky celebrates that jargon; it is the singing voice of the Yiddish poet, Yehoash, whose words are inwreathed

into parts of *A*, and into the 1926 'Poem Beginning "The" '. Yehoash's
writing career was continually concerned with the problem of the relation of Yiddish to Hebrew, and one of his major projects was to compile
a dictionary which was intended to demonstrate the connections
between the two.[33] That synthesis, a demonstration in writing of a
harmony out of deep division, would have had Zukofsky's sympathy as
it is analogous to the movement of all his own poetry. The son learns
from the father and, having put aside hostility, allows his own labour to
flower. This is speech growing to song, which is indeed how Zukofsky
describes his intended project in *A* (e.g. A 138).

A 1-12 may be seen, then, as the working out of a particular mode
of writing from within the context of Poundian influence, in so far as
Pound can be viewed as a symbolic father, the immediate poetic
ancestor of *A*. The poem follows a process of 'ecdysis' (A 2), always
wishing to throw off the antagonisms and stultifications of the political
world in which the father is so heavily involved, and thence present the
liveforever form that can pass beyond the Poundian gaze: indeed, to
emulate him to the point of being able to tell him:

> Have your odyssey
> How many voiced it be
> Speak to me in a different anguish (A 128).

The different anguish is to be that of following the course of desire,
hazardous (in Mallarméan terms) as it is, but in any case accepting the
death of the father, mourning the phallus as Lacan says, and facing up
to the scar of the subject's own self-sacrifice, of his loss, his death
which is the beginning of writing.

Access to desire is gained at a price, then, the price of the recognition
of the subject's splitting, his fundamental condition of being out of phase
with the real. For Lacan, as for Freud, this splitting is set upon the bedrock of the death-drive. The gap in the subject is symbolised by Lacan
by the *objet a*, a cipher of otherness and the object that the subject has
lost 'and will not find . . . again until he sacrifices himself'.[34] It is that
sacrificial and deferential gesture that Zukofsky's texts undertake. His
writing occurs within the context of his own death, the erasure of his
name. Just as Hume's autobiography, which Zukofsky admired, speaks
in the past tense ('I was a man of cheerful disposition . . . '),[35] so
'A-18' begins with 'it is I who have died' (A 389). Such an erasure is
effected in the interests of the text itself: it is no longer the man him-

self but 'the song preserves/recurring saves us' (A 393).

We are told that Zukofsky was a great hypochondriac.[36] The song, in its preserving role, is capable of compensating for the disappearance, the death of the ego; and that the song might act as a manifestation of Zukofsky's feelings of love and amity is corroborated by Freud's statement that 'a strong egoism is a protection against falling ill, but in the last resort we must begin to love in order not to fall ill'. Freud goes on to quote Heine (which I relay in Strachey's translation):

> God is imagined as saying: 'Illness was no doubt the final cause of the whole urge to create. By creating I could recover; by creating I became healthy.'[37]

Zukofsky is that sort of creator, a man who 'sits down with an aspirin without a prayer' (A 393) to formulate the 'hernia of a book' (A 394), or 'eight words a line for love' (A 393).

Thus the text of *A* is constituted by the hypochondriacal attachment of the libido to words in a recognition of the body and its desire: it is a working-out of that desire. Zukofsky's is that 'organ-speech'[38] that Freud makes note of, a libidinal attachment to words as an expression of the erotogenicity of the body. To put it in another way, as Zukofsky does, 'the word is so much of a physiological thing': it has 'articulation' ('words have knees') that 'will make an object'.[39] The complete *A*, indeed, acts as the hallucination for the lost object which only death or the sacrifice of all narcissistic attachments can recover for the subject. In its recognition of the subject's split it takes its primary poetic strategy from Freud's insight that in such fantasies (Lacan calls them 'phallophanies')[40] it is the 'sameness of the words used' to express things, rather than the identity of things, which dictates the shapes of utterance.[41]

Such a strategy is, of course, metonymic, the course of language's desire, and it is a strategy always at play in Zukofsky. 'A-22' and 'A-23', in fact, are seemingly motivated by

> a nerve's aching respond to
> energies not itself . . .
> sings sometimes, thoughts' template
> somehow furthers a cento reading (A 535)

— that is to say, motivated by the energy of language in the body. The particulars and complexities of the world are imposed upon the body through 'thoughts' template', through the structure of language which somehow must be allowed to express what it will, the plurality of 'a cento reading'. The light-hearted 'comedy' of that process, set against what is 'tragic' in the fixity of conventional thought, is allegorised by the description of the gardener amongst his flowers:

> a peasant gardener's attentions, blossoms
>
> he greets by ancient names
> 'iberis prefers limestone — evonymus prospers'
> no twenty-two reasons argue them —
> unurged aptness untallied sunned the
> comedy's divine, tragic a Thought.

The gardener's joyful naming of his flowers establishes their complex plurality without the intrusion or interruption of the trammels of rationality: after all, it is language's idiosyncrasies that make

> ... black hellebore
> (or winter rose) white literally
> (botanically not a rose) ...

The pleasure the gardener takes in the irrational offerings of language, the enjoyment of the gaps between words and things is accompanied by his cynicism towards all sorts of epistemology and his preference for the eye as an entrance to the world — but not the idealist's eye, rather an eye that differentiates, learns otherness from the world. Zukofsky's poem is liberatedly self-conscious in a way which allows language entirely to guide the sense of his utterance. 'Sounds are too volatile for legal restraint' (A 395) and lead the writer to areas of language that are characterised by the something more that I have talked about — materiality in all its exuberance, excess and surplus. 'Names have often many ideas, few ideas have names' (A 395). The project has, in fact, been named in a slightly ironical way, in one of Zukofsky's shorter poems:

> For you I have emptied the meaning
> Leaving the song.[42]

This is, of course, necessarily ironic since even in the prosecution of that statement, a meaning is proffered. That short poem includes, once again, the speaking voice partially converted and awaiting the coming of the 'singing gut'. In the performance of the aspired song meaning obviously cannot be totally 'emptied', but utterance can learn how to cut across, semiotically, the structures of fixed meaning, at least to question its rigidity. In such a strategy a musical analogy is always implicit: the metonymic flow provides the text with *motif* and *theme* which, like their musical counterparts, do not have a given meaning, but serve to guide the movement and topical incidences of the text. A passage from 'A-18' (A 396-401) will show what I mean by this.

Much of 'A-18' is stimulated by thoughts of American imperialism as it makes its invasions on Korea, Vietnam and on to the moon. In an antithesis that would be familiar to H.D., Zukofsky explores the accidents of language's roots in the name of one of the instruments of that imperialist aggression – napalm. Napalm bombs are constructed, from a mixture of petrol (napthenic) and coconut (palmitic) acids, to produce fire: the napalm gel is manufactured by freezing the mixture, a cryobiological process. Zukofsky, exploiting the consonances of 'the exuberance of words' (A 395), their fruitful abundance, is led to his meditations by the word's palmitic root, by the notion of burning and scorching, and by that of freezing.

The effect of napalm is to leave us 'no palm' (A 396), or assuming the argotic boxing term 'coconut', no heads: not only the Vietnamese but the Americans too have lost their heads by the production of this bomb (itself like a coconut, a solid shell broken to release a liquid) made by the uprooting of plants for the uprooting of human beings. Zukofsky is reminded of 'manroot' (A 396) and the legend of its forked (A-like, man-like) roots shrieking as they are pulled from the ground. The weeping that napalm's scorching action causes is linked with cryobiology – the scientific process being used in this case to make us cry in 'cryochore' (A 399) – cry, o heart – all over the world. Cryochore is itself, of course, the mode of St Matthew's Passion, the performance of which at Carnegie Hall had begun *A*. Christ's passion is further evoked by the 'self-immolation of roger allen la porte' in protest at the Vietnam war: La Porte was a 'seminarian briefed *chrystie* street where I was born' (A 399, my emphasis).

Thus, by any number of roots, the language brings napalm home to where care and attention to the roots, the 'umbilical chord' (A 399) of humanity can remain effective – though still painful – in its enactment:

> my love scorched as she watched the self-immolation . . .
> . . . only in my love's
> room did the plants not burn: in world's
> hangar great room honesty a shade gray
> the unminded plant burned with all others (A 399).

It is in the microcosmic space of the home that language must begin to be nurtured for its role of demonstrating how, in Stokes' words, 'to keep the good alive amid so many dangers'.[43] And we know who is producing the dangers, and how.

Zukofsky's notions of how the root can be exploited are thus massively different from Pound's. For Zukofsky, the root is in language and language's roots (its etymologies and phonologies) which grow metonymically, unhalted by any 'plan' such as Pound's: 'Words (are)/hourly shifting' (A 395), not tied to signifieds, and they should be in this respect analogous to our own bodies, ours to shift along the blood flow. Whereas in the interests of universal order Pound is led to make a metaphorical collocation of body and state, Zukofsky's metonymic explorations of the umbilical cords of language point to a relation of excess between the individual, his language and social organisation: metonymic links present a scheme in language which is ignored by the state; they make a demonstration of 'intricacy' set against 'the weight' of fixity (A 344). As a demonstration of this on a very simple level, Zukofsky removes himself from the social organism in which he finds himself by demonstrating a different and more generous use of the roots of the coconut. Indeed, in the Melanesian and Trobriander legends that Zukofsky explores, the coconut is used variously as a staple food for subsistence, and as a sort of symbolic guarantee for the return of the dead; its leaves are used to cradle an almost Kleinian 'new life' and its eyes are used to allow the dead to see their way to a return to life. The eyes of the coconut, and its leaves, are, as it were, the very movement of Zukofsky's text which would wish to act in a similar revivifying process. In short, what the word 'coconut' has supplied for Zukofsky is an alternative example to the misappropriation of people and objects by the modes of Western civilisation. The word stands against the object; language stands against the (political) reality that produces the horrors of a bomb designed to uphold — by the destruction of difference — the fixed modes of that reality.

It is tempting to read, in this context, Zukofsky's anecdote about a 'Miraculous Fish' (A 392) found in a Vietnam pond and used as a sort of totemic symbol by the Buddhists and peasants of the area, as a sort of

allegory of language's situation. The giant fish might be language itself.
It is attacked by the Americans' 'automatic weapons . . . hand grenades
. . . terrific explosions' and yet 'the fish officially "continued" to
swim'.

I take it that it is quite clear from the example of Zukofsky's
method that I have chosen that *A* must be regarded as a political poem,
both in its overt propositions and in its general linguistic strategies. In
the latter of these two characteristics, at least, it resembles *Finnegans
Wake*. *A*'s demonstrable provenance in Pound's work leaves it, however,
with more overt signs of a concern with the relation between the
economic/political real and language than Joyce allows his text to display. It is perhaps the fact that Zukofsky's work often has a topical
pretext, just as Pound's has in a more generalised way, that marks him
off from Joyce: even in the writing which I take to be closest to Joyce's
Zukofsky uses a pre-text. I am thinking of his versions of Catullus and
of 'A-21' which is itself a version of Plautus' *Rudens*. It is in such
writing that, as Charles Tomlinson has noticed, 'he had pushed what he
called "the noise" of poetry about as far as it would go'. Like most
critics Tomlinson is wary of Zukofsky's 'transliterations' (even in that
description a disapproval of Zukofsky's transgressions can be glimpsed),
but he recognises that 'it was not only Pound that lay behind his ven-
ture, but principally the Joyce of *Finnegans Wake*'.[44] Thus Zukofsky's
work can be seen as a sort of unholy marriage of those two great and
influential figures of twentieth-century literature, acting in an interstice
between them, or beginning with one and ending with the other.

What Zukofsky has done more consistently than either Joyce or
Pound (despite Pound's attacks on him) is to involve his project with
the topical events of his day — race riots, the death of John Kennedy,
the Depression, the wars that America was involved in this century, the
moon-shots, the Cold War and so on. All this in his attempt to supply
'the common air'; but most importantly he has followed in Joyce's
path rather than Pound's by giving the materiality of language full rein
to deal with these things. If that project is undertaken from a secure
home base it is no less effective for that, as he relates the qualities and
characteristics of that base to the divided state of humanity, attempting to offer suggestions as to why that division should and could be
transformed to harmony. In answer to critics like Mottram and Heller
(whose arguments in fact would have the effect of denying efficacy to
any sort of art), and in response to Zukofsky's own wife telling me
that 'Louis was totally apolitical'[45] (and also against the implicit and
similar judgement that resides behind the *Paideuma* adoption of Zukof-

sky as Pound's true heir) I would be inclined to propose Christopher Middleton's poem, 'How to Listen to Birds':[46] Zukofsky has 'put no trust in loud sounds' such as the ones Pound produces, and has found a way

> To speak
> Belief, at a variance so fine
> It modifies the whole
>
> Machine of being: this
> Is not unpolitical.

Middleton is one of those contemporary poets whose work might have acted, had this book been extended, as the locus for a further exploration of the tensions between the semiotic and the symbolic as I have used those terms. His work explores exactly the tensions occurring between the body and language that I have been concerned with. He talks of language in the same terms as does Zukofsky: it is a 'wave creation', a somatic response to the 'concentration et l'évaporation du Moi',[47] or the linguistic mark of the unconscious as it pulsates in a movement of dehiscence and closure.

Middleton typifies such an 'intent listening to the wave' as 'a purely European passion'[48] but of course, the whole movement of Zukofsky's American poem is exactly this. One of its most evident manifestations in *A* is probably 'A-19' (A 408 ff) which is constructed in a 'down up' movement of stanzas designed to represent the movement of Paul Zukofsky's bow over his violin.[49] But it also represents the systolic and diastolic pulsion of the heart pumping the blood — it is, after all, an 'encore', another song in and by the heart. It is also the up and down movement of coition and thus creation, so it not accidentally deals with the next generation, with the creation of the poem, or music, from the particulars of the world.

'A-19' is focused upon a violin competition in which Paul Zukofsky took part in 1965. The element of chance that the competition enjoins, and the memory of a present of Mallarmé's work that Paul made to his father, provoke Mallarmé's entry into the text as the hazardous poet of 'Un Coup de Des . . . ': Mallarmé's influence adds other layers to the dyadic partition of the stanzas — he installs, for example, the antitheses of black ink on white paper, one of his continual motifs which also is reminiscent of Zukofsky's dealings with the race riots of the sixties in 'A-15'. Mallarmé also provokes the notion of 'two/sides of a coin'

(A 429), and the endless permutations and unpredictabilities of language's exuberance.

From Mallarmé, too, comes the poem's social setting. First, his hope
that

> the crowd
> other than
> by silence
> takes part
> exults as
> choir . . . voices . . . vaults (A 426)

in the production of his work. Second, some of Mallarmé's reflections
on the way 'to/feed young/artists' by taxation of the rich feed the
poem's interest in the son: Zukofsky's deference to his son and wife's
musical ability is the whole of *A*'s concern as speech grows into song, in
the harmony of son and father with 'bowed Heart' (A 409). Inscribed
into 'A-19' too are many of Mallarmé's words, most importantly parts
of his 'Chansons Bas', little verses about workers and their families:

> . . . woman
> child broth
> quarryman cut out
>
> for his
> marriage cobbler
> shoes (feet)
> if you
> will revive
> everyday's amities (A 410).

It is the revivification of amity and solidarity with people whose labour
is exploited that *A* generally intends.

The poem is also set within the remembrance that Mallarmé himself
suffered the loss of his own son, who died while young, and – a recognition of a different order – that 'A-19' is being written near 'the 20th/
anniversary of Hiroshima's A'. These two events cast their shadow over
the poem as they are linked with Zukofsky's thoughts of his own son
who provides

A legacy
windfall of
a rush
of notes (A 433).

(The windfall is, of course, the atomic fall-out as well as a piece of luck,
and the notes are a means of subsistence as well as music.) The universal application of the processes of creation and inheritance, linked thus
with death and subsistence, place the making of the poem in that tension of home and world that I have spoken of. It is only by *chance* that
Zukofsky finds himself in his given position, able to pay attention to
the way in which language works in opposition to the horrific products
of men's attempts to impose order (the bomb, or the *Cantos*) on other
men. The only mode of activity open to the creative gardener is to ensure, by careful attention to the language's flowers,that the song grows
up so that

... From
thence sorrow
be ever
raz'd. (A 434)

Or, as he puts it elsewhere, less ironically, as the old de-compose we
should 'venerate our young' (A 278).

Coda

As to the young: 'The French take their hats off to them,' as to the
dead (A 278), in a gesture of equality and deference. It is interesting to
note that Mallarmé regarded the top hat as 'a black egalitarian plat-
form', an instrument which, as Thomas Hanson points out,[50] because of
its ambiguous sexual symbolism (it is a sort of pineal eye, vertically
phallic, ending in the feminine O at the top), acts to displace the
overtly paternal modes of most headgear! Mallarmé considers that it is a
hat to 'mow down diadems and tresses' and so disrupt the power of patriarchal structures. And, of course,

Wherever
we put
our hats

is our
home (A 424)

the end, z-sited, point of the epic journey, a place ruled over by love
and song rather than by the paternal Logos, and the haven of attention
to the language as it performs

in favour
of all
the world
restored to
the people (A 424)

From the age of three to the age of five, Gargantua was brought up and disciplined in all the necessary ways, such being his father's orders; and he spent that time in the same way as the other children of the area: that's to say, in drinking, eating and sleeping.

He was always rolling in the mud, dirtying his nose, scratching his face, and treading down his shoes; and he often gaped after flies, or ran happily after the butterflies of whom his father was ruler. He pissed in his shoes, shat in his shirt, wiped his nose on his sleeve, snivelled into his food, paddled about all over the place, drank out of his shoes, and rubbed his belly on food baskets. He sharpened his teeth on shoe-leather, washed his hands in soup, combed his hair with a wine-bowl, sat between two stools with his bum on the ground, covered himself with wet sacks, sucked while eating his soup, ate his biscuits without bread, bit as he laughed and laughed as he bit, often spat in his dish, blew a big fart, pissed against the sun, ducked underwater to avoid the rain, struck the iron while it was cold, had empty thoughts, put on airs, vomited his food or, so they say, flayed the fox, mumbled his prayers like an ape, returned to his muttons, and turned the pigs out to hay. He would beat the dog in front of the lion, put the cart before the horse, scratch where he wasn't itching, pull the worms out of his nose, grip so hard that he caught nothing, eat the white bread first, shoe grass-hoppers, and tickle himself till he laughed. He was a great guzzler in the kitchen, offered the gods straw for grain, sang Magnificats at matins and thought this the right time, ate cabbages and shat beets, found the flies in his milk and pulled their legs off, scrawled on paper, blotted parchment, got away by his heels, played ducks and drakes with his purse, reckoned without his host, beat the bushes and missed the birds, and took the clouds for brass frying-pans and bladders for lanterns. He would draw two loads from one sack, play the donkey to get the bran, use his fist as a mallet, take cranes at the first leap, think a coat of mail was made link by link, always look a gift horse in the mouth, ramble from cock to bull, put a ripe fruit between two green, make the best of a bad job, protect the moon from the wolves, hope to catch larks if the heavens fell, take a slice of any bread he was offered, care as little for the bald as the shaven, and flay the fox every morning. His father's dogs ate out of his bowl and he ate with them. He bit their ears and they scratched his nose; he blew up their bums and they licked his lips.

And you know what, lads? That little lecher was always feeling his governess, upside down, back to front, and any way at all. He was already beginning to exercise his cod-piece, which his governesses decorated each day with garlands, fine ribbons, pretty flowers and gay silks. And they amused themselves by rubbing it between their hands like a roll of pastry and then burst out laughing when it pricked its ears, as if the game pleased them. One of them called it my pillicock, another my ninepin, another my coral-branch, another my stopper, my cork, my quiverer, my driving-pin, my oracle, my dingle-dangle, my stiff-and-low, my crimping iron, my little red sausage, my sweet little cock.

It's mine, said one. It belongs to me, another. What about me, a third. Don't I get a bit? I shall cut it off then.

What? said another. Cut it off, that would hurt him, Madam. Is that what you do with children's things? Why, then he's Master Short.

And so that he could enjoy himself like all the other kids of the area they made him a weathercock from the sails of a windmill.

NOTES

Chapter 1

1. Foreword to *A Lume Spento* (London, 1965), p. 7.
2. K.K. Ruthven, *A Guide to Ezra Pound's 'Personae' (1926)* (Berkeley, 1969).
3. T.H. Jackson, *The Early Poetry of Ezra Pound* (Cambridge, Mass., 1968), p. 128.
4. C. de Nagy, *The Poetry of Ezra Pound: the Pre-Imagist Stage* (Bern, 1968), p. 73.
5. Arthur Symons, *Silhouettes* (London, 1892), pp. 3-10.
6. Arthur Symons, *Dramatis Personae* (Indianapolis, 1896), p. 343.
7. A.C. Swinburne, *Poems and Ballads (1st Series)* (London, 1896), p. 145.
8. V. Forrest-Thomson, 'Open and Closed Verse' (unpublished).
9. T.S. Eliot, *The Sacred Wood* (London, 1972), p. 150.
10. 'How I Began', *T.P.'s Weekly* 6 June 1913, p. 707.
11. A. Crozier, 'The Young Pound', *PN Review*, vol. 5, no. 2, pp. 27-8.
12. R. Duncan, 'The Lasting Contribution of Ezra Pound', *Agenda*, vol. 4, no. 2, p. 25.
13. D. Davie, *The Poet as Sculptor* (London, 1964), p. 246.
14. *Money Pamphlets by £*, no. 6 (London, 1951).
15. 'How I Began', p. 707.
16. 'Two Notes', *Egoist*, 1 June 1915, pp. 88-9.
17. 'Rhythm and Imagery in English Poetry', *British Journal of Aesthetics* (January 1962).
18. 'Pound's Wordsworth', *ELH*, vol. 45, no. 4, p. 662.
19. Quoted by S. Coffman, *Imagism* (New York, 1972), p. 176.

Chapter 2

1. 'The Approach to Paris, I', *New Age*, 4 September 1913, pp. 551-2, and 'America: Chances and Remedies', *New Age*, vol. 13, p. 58.
2. *New Age*, vol. 13, p. 83.
3. C. Seely (ed.), *Charles Olson and Ezra Pound: an Encounter at St Elizabeths* (New York, 1975), p. 90.
4. 'Piers Plowman in the Modern Wasteland in N. Stock (ed.), *Perspectives* (Chicago, 1965), pp. 154-76.
5. P. Whigham, 'Ezra Pound and Catullus', *Perspectives*, p. 74.
6. *Le Degré Zéro de l'Ecriture* (Paris, 1972), p. 7.
7. See D.Davie, *The Poet as Sculptor* (London, 1964), p. 97.
8. Ibid., p. 93.
9. *New Bearings in English Poetry* (London, 1950), p. 235.
10. D. Davie, *Poet as Sculptor*, p. 136.
11. S. Fender, *The American Long Poem: an Annotated Selection* (London,

1977), pp. 94-109.

12. C. Emery, *Ideas Into Action* (Miami, 1958), p. 33.

13. Quoted by S. Coffman, *Imagism* (New York, 1972), p. 119.

14. Quoted by Coffman, ibid., p. 55.

15. *The Class Struggles in France, 1848-1850* (New York, 1972), p. 53.

16. *A Draft of XVI Cantos* (Three Mountains Press edition, 1925).

17. See J. Drummond's account in P. Russell (ed.), *An Examination of Ezra Pound* (New York, 1973), p. 112n.

18. Ibid., p. 112.

19. E.P. Nassar, *The Cantos of Ezra Pound: the Lyric Mode* (Johns Hopkins, 1975), p. 29.

20. See E.H. Gombrich, 'Icones Symbolicae', *Journal of the Warburg and Courtauld Institutes*, vol. 11 (1948).

Chapter 3

1. M. Sinclair, 'Two Notes', *The Egoist*, 1 June 1915, p. 88.

2. D. Davie, *The Poet as Sculptor* (London, 1964), p. 173.

3. 'The Rock Drill' in N. Stock (ed.), *Perspectives* (Chicago, 1965), p. 199.

4. See B. MacNaughton, 'Pound: a Brief Memoir', *Paideuma*, vol. 3, p. 323.

5. C.F. Terrell, *Paideuma*, vol. 2, p. 80.

6. Davie, *Poet as Sculptor, passim*, but especially pp. 127-31 and 155-6.

7. See A. Stokes, *Critical Writings* (3 vols., London, 1978), especially vol. 1.

8. Quoted in E. Mottram, 'Pound, Olson and the Golden Flower', *Chapman* (Summer 1972), p. 27.

9. See D. Gordon, for example, 'The Azalea is Grown', *Paideuma*, vol. 4, p. 223.

10. G. Dekker, *Sailing after Knowledge* (London, 1963), pp. 126-8.

11. H. Kenner (ed.), *The Translations of Ezra Pound* (London, 1963), p. 23.

12. J.J. Wilhelm, *The Later Cantos of Ezra Pound* (New York, 1977), p. 22.

13. Stokes, *The Critical Writings*, vol. 1, p. 230.

14. Ibid., p. 230-1.

15. Ibid., p. 231.

16. S. Freud, *The Standard Edition of the Complete Psychological Works* (24 vols. London, 1951), vol. 7, p. 221.

17. Telegram to the editors of *Paideuma* (vol. 6, pp. 415-16). The unfortunate butt of Ms Martinelli's spleen was René Odlin who in vol. 6, pp. 181-2, had the audacity to attempt 'to diminish Mr Pound's respectability as a subject for academic exercises'.

18. See Chapter 6.

19. Wilhelm, *Later Cantos*, pp. 20-34.

20. C.D. Heymann, *Ezra Pound: the Last Rower* (London, 1976), p. 301.

21. C. Brooke-Rose, *A ZBC of Ezra Pound* (London, 1971), pp. 90ff.

22. M.L. Rosenthal, 'Pound at his best: Canto 47 as a model of poetic thought', *Paideuma*, vol. 6, pp. 309-21. That essay also appears in *Sailing into the Unknown* (Oxford, 1978). The article which I wrote in conjunction with A.E. Durant (of which some of the present chapter is a reworking) was designed as some sort of rebuttal of Rosenthal's article. See P.H. Smith and A.E. Durant, 'Pound's Metonymy: Canto 47 Revisited', *Paideuma*, vol. 8, pp. 327-33.

23. W. Pearlman, *The Barb of Time* (Oxford, 1969), p. 171.

24. See Wilhelm, *Later Cantos*, p. 87.

25. J.H. Edwards and W.V. Vasse, *Annotated Index to Cantos 1-84* (Berkeley, 1957), p. 3.

26. Letters, pp. 131-2.

27. *Paideuma*, vol. 5, pp. 15-29. See R. Jakobson, *Selected Writings* (Hague, 1971), vol. 2, pp. 239-52.

28. J. Lacan, *Ecrits* (Paris, 1966), p. 14.

29. See Lacan, ibid., pp. 505-9.

30. Lacan quoted and translated by A. Wilden, *The Language of the Self* (New York, 1968), p. 242.

31. Lacan, *Ecrits*, p. 853.

32. H. Schneidau, 'Wisdom Past Metaphor', *Paideuma*, vol. 5, no. 1, p. 15.

33. Homer, *The Odyssey* (London, 1963), p. 163.

34. 'The Music of a Lost Dynasty: Pound in the Classroom', *Boston University Journal* (Winter 1972), p. 38.

35. Davie, *Poet as Sculptor*, p. 225.

36. Schneidau, 'Wisdom Past Metaphor', p. 22.

37. Letter quoted with permission from the original manuscript in the Lilly Library, Indiana University, Bloomington.

38. M. Reck, 'A Conversation between Ezra Pound and Allen Ginsberg', *Evergreen Review*, no. 57 (June 1968), pp. 27ff.

39. 'Pound's Progress in the Pisan Cantos', *Paideuma*, vol. 4, p. 77.

40. *Translations*, p. 21.

41. E. Fenollosa, *The Chinese Written Character as a Medium for Poetry* (San Francisco, City Lights edition, n. d.), p. 22.

42. Ibid., p. 12.

43. Ibid., p. 23.

44. Ezra Pound and the French Language, in Stock, *Perspectives*, p. 144.

45. See, for example, *New Age*, 11 Sept. 1913, p. 577.

46. This present chapter has been primarily stimulated by Derrida's *La Dissémination* (Paris, 1972) and its discussion of Plato's *Phaedrus*, 'La Pharmacie de Platon'.

47. Letters, p. 342. See Heymann, *Last Rower*, pp. 92-3.

48. C. MacCabe, *James Joyce and the Revolution of the Word* (London, 1977), p. 77.

49. Fenollosa, *Chinese Written Character*, p. 12.

50. Schneidau, 'Wisdom Past Metaphor', p. 16.

51. M. Nanny, *Poetics for an Electric Age* (Bern, 1973), p. 85.

52. M. Nänny, 'Oral Dimensions in Ezra Pound', *Paideuma*, vol. 6, pp. 13-26.

53. See V. Allenton, *Tel Quel*, no. 48/9, pp. 47ff, and H. Jensen, *Sign, Symbol and Script* (London, 1970).

54. Quoted by Nänny in *Electric Age*, p. 22.

55. Ibid., p. 73.

Chapter 4

1. R. Hofstadter, *The Age of Reform* (New York, 1961), pp. 62-77.

2. H.N. Smith, *The Virgin Land* (New York, 1950), p. 138.

3. See Hofstadter, *Age of Reform*, and Smith, *Virgin Land, passim*.

4. Apart from Hofstadter and Smith, see I.H. Herron, *The Small Town in American Literature* (New York, 1959); L. Ziff, *The American 1890's* (London, 1967); H. Jackson, *The 1890's* (London, 1922): these all deal with this and other

matters relevant to the present chapter.

5. Smith, *Virgin Land*, p. 179.

6. J.J. Wilhelm, *The Later Cantos of Ezra Pound* (New York, 1977), p. 49.

7. W. Reich, *The Mass Psychology of Fascism* (New York, 1970), p. 51.

8. Hofstadter, *Age of Reform*, p. 59.

9. Ibid., pp. 91-3.

10. Ibid., p. 33.

11. Franklin, quoted by Hofstadter, *Age of Reform*, p. 27.

12. R.W. Emerson, 'Nature', *Collected Works*, vol. 1 (Cambridge, Mass., 1971), p. 11.

13. S. Freud, *The Standard Edition of the Complete Psychological Works* (24 vols., London, 1951), vol. 21, p. 227.

14. W. Chace, *The Political Identities of Ezra Pound and T.S. Eliot* (Stanford, 1973), pp. 33 and 64.

15. Reich, *Mass Psychology*, p. 62-3.

16. M. Reck, *Ezra Pound: a Close-up* (London, 1968), Introduction. The ambiguity of the word 'close-up' should become apparent in the present chapter.

17. Pound interviewed by D. Hall, *Paris Review*, no. 28, p. 38.

18. Reck, *Close-up*, p. 6.

19. See PD, p. 10, where this transformation first occurs. Later, Homer Pound is translated to 'the naive Euripides Weight' (PD 15). The aggressively phallic possibilities of the forename, too, are brought out when Euripides is shortened to Rip.

20. J.W. Scott, quoted by Smith, *Virgin Land*, p. 186.

21. Reich, *Mass Psychology*, p. 46.

22. Reck, *Close-up*, p. 4.

23. C.D. Heymann, *Ezra Pound: the Last Rower* (London, 1976), p. 7.

24. *Paris Review* interview, p. 39.

25. *Tel Quel*, no. 70, pp. 11ff. Following E. Langumier's recommendation of 'a new type of Poundian criticism based on the analysis of analerotic representations in Pound's work' (*Paideuma*, vol. 8, p. 57), and using similar sorts of critical and psychoanalytical approaches as Pleynet's, are M. Ellmann's 'Floating the Pound', *Oxford Literary Review*, vol. 3, no. 3, pp. 16-32, and A.E. Durant's *Ezra Pound: Identity in Crisis* (Brighton, 1981): and, of course, the present chapter.

26. N. Stock, *The Life of Ezra Pound* (London, 1974), pp. 11-12.

27. Pleynet, *Tel Quel*, p. 25, quoting an article by I. Fonagy in *Révue Française de Psychanalyse* (janvier 1970).

28. *Paris Review* interview, p. 39.

29. Freud, *Standard Edition*, vol. 9, p. 172.

30. Ibid., p. 174.

31. E. Bornemann, *The Psychoanalysis of Money* (New York, 1976), p. 49.

32. *Paris Review* interview, p. 40.

33. Ellmann quotes Lacan's *Four Fundamental Concepts of Psychoanalysis* (London, 1979), p. 104.

34. Freud, *Standard Edition*, vol. 9, p. 169.

35. *Paris Review* interview, p. 40

36. Durant, *Identity in Crisis*, (Brighton, 1981), p. 138.

37. Emerson, 'Nature', p. 19 (my emphasis).

38. Ibid., p. 23.

39. Ibid., p. 9.

40. Ibid., p. 43.

41. Ibid., p. 10.

42. Ibid., p. 10.
43. See Lacan, *Four Fundamental Concepts*, especially pp. 67-119.

Chapter 5

1. 'The Mathematical Symbolism of Ezra Pound's Revolutionary Mind', *Paideuma*, vol. 7, pp. 7-72; now part of his book *'76: One World and the 'Cantos'* (North Carolina, 1981).
2. G. Bataille, *Oeuvres Complètes*, vol. 2 (Paris, 1970), p. 96.
3. Jeffrey Mehlman, *Revolution and Repetition* (Berkeley, 1977), p. 25; J. Derrida, *Glas* (Paris, 1974), p. 7.
4. *The 18th Brumaire of Louis Bonaparte* (New York, 1963), p. 19.
5. Bataille, *Oeuvres*, vol. 2, p. 96.
6. J. Derrida, *Writing and Difference* (London, 1978), p. 294.
7. F. Read (ed.), *Pound/Joyce* (London, 1967), pp. 35 and 58.
8. Quoted with permission from the original manuscript in the Lilly Library, Indiana University, Bloomington. Seldes was, at this time, editor of *The Dial*.

The path that my argument will follow is sketched out in Roland Barthes' recent book on photography, *La Chambre Claire* (Paris, 1980). Talking of precisely this concern that the subject of a photograph feels about his relation to his image, Barthes says:

> I want my image, mobile, jostled among a thousand changing photos, at the behest of situations or age, to always coincide with my 'me' (and its profundity); but we should be saying the opposite: that 'me' never coincides with my image; because it's the 'me' that is flighty, immobile, obstinate, dispersed and, like a Cartesian diver, doesn't stay in a fixed position. (pp. 26-7)

9. J. Lacan, *The Four Fundamental Concepts of Psychoanalysis* (London, 1979), p. 29.
10. Ibid., p. 82.
11. Ibid., p. 22.
12. *Pound/Joyce*, p. 256.
13. S. Gilbert (ed.), *The Letters of James Joyce* (London, 1957), p. 220.
14. *Pound/Joyce*, p. 85.
15. Ibid., p. 96.
16. Ibid., p. 85.
17. Ibid., p. 91.
18. Ibid., p. 92.
19. R. Ellmann (ed.), *The Letters of James Joyce* (London, 1966), vol. 3, p. 146.
20. *Pound/Joyce*, p. 144.
21. Ibid.
22. Ibid., p. 256.
23. Lacan, *Four Fundamental Concepts*, p. 47.
24. R. Ellmann, *James Joyce* (Oxford, 1959), p. 559.
25. *Pound/Joyce*, p. 256.
26. Ibid.
27. *Autobiography* (New York, 1967), p. 51.
28. *Imaginations* (New York, 1971), p. 355.

29. Ibid., p. 357.

30. Bataille, *Oeuvres*, vol. 2, p. 18.

31. Ibid., p. 19.

32. Ibid., p. 15.

33. *Pound/Joyce*, p. 106. Wells's remark about 'cloacal obsession' is quoted on p. 94.

34. Ibid., p. 131.

35. Ibid., p. 157.

36. Ibid., p. 158.

37. Not a great deal of Kristeva's work is available in English but what there is is extremely valuable: 'The Semiotic Activity', *Screen*, vol. 14, no. 1/2, pp. 25-39; 'Signifying Practice and the Mode of Production', *Edinburgh Magazine*, no. 1. G. Howell-Smith's introduction to the latter article is especially useful. Some of Kristeva's more recent work has been collected in *Desire in Language* (New York, 1980).

38. Ellmann, *James Joyce*, p. 469.

39. Ibid., p. 705. Joyce was always intrigued by such accidents and coincidences: for example, the over-determined picture of Cork that he hung in his Paris flat – it was framed in cork (Ellmann, *James Joyce*, p. 563).

40. Ibid., p. 469.

41. See *Pound/Joyce*, pp. 301-2, where Pound's editing, reductive desires are allowed to play on precisely a scene of anal laxity.

42. 'Trames de la lecture', *Tel Quel*, no. 54.

43. S. Becket (ed.), *Our Exagmination etc* (London, 1972), p. 149.

44. *James Joyce and the Revolution of the Word* (London, 1977), p. 29.

45. *A Portrait of the Artist as a Young Man* (London, 1971), p. 188.

46. Ellmann, *James Joyce*, p. 646.

47. Ibid., p. 713.

48. Ibid., p. 565.

49. Ibid., p. 477.

50. Heath, 'Trames de la lecture', *passim.*

51. *Hermes to his Son Thoth* (Woodward, Penn, 1968), Ch. 4.

52. J. Lidderdale and M. Nicholson, *Dear Miss Weaver* (London, 1970), p. 336.

53. MacCabe, *Revolution of the Word* p. 156.

54. H. Levin has in fact characterised Joyce's work as the language of the outlaw in *James Joyce: a Critical Introduction* (London, 1960); and, of course, the theme of exile has been thoroughly dealt with by numerous critics.

55. Lidderdale and Nicholson, *Dear Miss Weaver*, p. 370.

56. *Life for Life's Sake* (London, 1968), p. 296.

57. *Shakespeare & Co.* (London, 1960), p. 188.

58. Lidderdale and Nicholson, *Dear Miss Weaver*, p. 328.

59. Ibid., p. 336.

60. This paragraph has owed much to MacCabe's work already cited. See, too, pp. 73-95 of R. Ellmann's *The Consciousness of Joyce* (London, 1977).

61. Quoted in S. Friedman's doctoral thesis on H.D., University of Wisconsin, 1976.

62. Ellmann, *James Joyce*, p. 538.

63. Ibid., p. 480.

64. See René Major's article, 'I am Joyce (Freud)' *Magazine Littéraire*, no. 161, pp. 41-2.

Chapter 6

1. Pound's unpublished letter to H.D. quoted by Norman Holmes Pearson in his foreword to *Tribute to Freud* (TF xiv). H.D.'s dream reported in TF, p. 152.

2. N. Stock, *The Life of Pound* (London, 1974), p. 121.

3. C. Norman, *Ezra Pound: a Biography* (London, 1969), pp. 5-6.

4. See Norman, ibid., p. 6 (even though he makes the mistake of calling H.D.'s father Eric, which was in fact the name of his son).

5. N.N. Holland, 'H.D. and the Blameless Physician', *Contemporary Literature*, vol. 10, no. 4, p. 486.

6. S. Freud, *The Standard Edition of the Complete Psychological Works* (24 vols., London, 1951), vol. 19, p. 179.

7. This paragraph relies on Lacan's seminar on the mirror stage, *Ecrits* (Paris, 1966), pp. 93-100, and on A. Lemaire's *Jacques Lacan* (London, 1977), p. 128.

8. M. Liebovici, 'La Position Féminine dans la Bible', *Tel Quel*, no. 75, pp. 100-1.

9. S. Leclaire, *Psychanalyser* (Paris, 1968), p. 72.

10. See Lemaire, *Jacques Lacan*, p. 144, and J. Laplanche and S. Leclaire, 'The Unconscious', *Yale French Studies*, no. 48.

11. Lemaire, *Jacques Lacan*, p. 149.

12. Holland, 'H.D.', p. 474.

13. *By Avon River* (New York, 1949), p. 6.

14. Ibid., p. 15.

15. Ibid., p. 16.

16. Ibid., p. 24.

17. *Red Roses for Bronze* (London, 1931), p. 18.

18. L. Mulvey and P. Wollen, 'The Riddles of the Sphinx: a script', *Screen*, vol. 18, no. 2, p. 75.

19. N.H. Pearson, 'An Interview on H.D.', *Contemporary Literature*, vol. 10, no. 4, p. 443; Bryher, *The Heart to Artemis* (London, 1962), p. 76.

20. Riddel, *The Inverted Bell* (Baton Rouge, 1974), p. 76.

21. Lemaire, *Jacques Lacan*, p, 138, quoting S. Leclaire. Freud on the mystic writing pad is in *Standard Edition*, vol. 19, pp. 227-34.

22. From 'Notes on Thought and Vision'.

23. In talking about Lacan's *Le Séminaire XX: Encore* (Paris, 1975), Stephen Heath locates Lacan's notion that the female may in some sense be identifiable with the unconscious: this is what I mean by essentialist feminism, found again in 'Riddles of the Sphinx' and elsewhere but convincingly reprimanded by Heath's article 'Difference', *Screen*, vol. 19, no. 3, pp. 50-116.

24. Liebovici, 'La Position Féminine', p. 101.

25. Mulvey and Wollen, 'Riddles of the Sphinx', p. 75.

26. V. Quinn, *Hilda Doolittle* (New York, 1967), p. 116.

27. In TF, p. 141, 'Stephen Guest brought me a copy of "The Man Who Died." He said, "Did you know that you are the priestess of Isis in this book?" ' H.D.'s relationship with Lawrence is the subject of much of TF's second part, 'Advent', though that book (and Lawrence's story) are conspicuously absent from P.E. Firchow's article, 'Rico and Julia: the Hilda Doolittle-D.H. Lawrence Affair Reconsidered', *JML* vol. 8, no. 1, pp. 51-76.

28. *The Tales of D.H. Lawrence* (London, 1934), p. 1120.

29. Ibid., p.1134.

30. Ibid., 1112.

31. Lacan, *Encore*, p. 70.

32. Heath, 'Difference', p. 78.
33. V. Quinn, 'H.D.'s "Hermetic Definition:" the Poet as Archetypal Mother', *Contemporary Literature*, vol. 18, no. 1, p. 59.
34. 'The Unconscious Structured as a Language', in C. MacCabe (ed.), *The Talking Cure* (London, 1981).
35. Letter of 5 September 1947, quoted by S.S. Friedman, 'Mythology, Psychoanalysis and the Occult in the Later Poetry of H.D.', PhD thesis, University of Wisconsin, 1973.
36. Quoted in N.H. Pearson's introduction to *Hermetic Definition* (Oxford, 1972).

Chapter 7

1. In fact, most of the earliest published notices of Zukofsky's work were by such poets as Rexroth, Creeley, Levertov, Williams, Niedecker.
2. After many years of commerce with Pound alone, *Paideuma* has devoted a special issue, vol. 7, no. 3, to Zukofsky, and now is attempting to 'explicate' his work in the same way as Pound's.
3. *An 'Objectivists' Anthology* (Le Beausset, Var, 1932).
4. Ibid., p. 27.
5. Ibid., p. 29.
6. Celia Zukofsky reports that Pound's death to Zukofsky was 'like losing a father', and she talks of the reverence and respect that Zukofsky felt for him. In an interview with C.F. Terrell, editor of *Louis Zukofsky: Man and Poet* (Orono, Maine, 1980), p. 74.
7. M. Booth, *Catalogue of LZ Collection* (HRC, Austin, Texas, 1975), p. 245. See also N. Stock, *The Life of Ezra Pound* (London, 1974), p. 397.
8. *Prepositions* (London, 1967), p. 157.
9. *The European*, vol. 22, no. 5, p. 284.
10. K. Cox, 'The Poetry of Louis Zukofsky', *Montemora*, no. 5, p. 8.
11. Booth, *LZ Collection*, p. 245.
12. Ibid.
13. *Prepositions*, p. 20.
14. Zukofsky's involvement in political activity on the left is, I think, quite likely, despite the repeated denials by Celia Zukofsky that her husband was ever politically active. One might imagine that his friendship with Whittaker Chambers, for example, would have involved him in such political activity. Certainly Zukofsky was investigated by the FBI concerning the Chambers-Hiss trial. For Celia Zukofsky's version of the story, see *Man and Poet*, pp. 50-1.
15. *Autobiography* (New York, 1970), p. 53.
16. E. Mottram, *Maps*, no. 5, pp. 94 and 97.
17. M. Heller, *Maps*, no. 5, p. 24.
18. Barry Ahearn, 'Materials for Collage', *ELH*, vol. 45, no. 1, p. 161.
19. Ibid., p. 169.
20. See *Bottom: On Shakespeare*, vol. 1 (Austin, Texas, 1963), p. 116.
21. The Gilgamesh story is, of course, precisely concerned with the harmony that arises from divisions; Zukofsky's story of Stronger and Strongest is to be found in A 540-543. The image of the city also strongly pervades later parts of 'A-23'.
22. It might be said that *A* fulfils Pound's failed projected poem based on a fugal structure in that it actually does conform to a more strictly imposed 'musical' form and procedure than anything in the *Cantos*. The question of

Notes

165

Zukofsky and form is an interesting one, and some of his thoughts about the imposition of form relate well to my first chapters on Pound: he seems to believe that the 'exuberance of words' can and should be channelled into a container, not for the ensuing imposition of a message, but precisely for the foregrounding of the language itself.

23. R. Barthes, *Image/Music/Text* (London, 1977), p. 142.

24. I owe this observation to W. Harmon's article, 'Eiron Eyes', *Parnassus* (Spring/Summer 1979). See *An 'Objectivists' Anthology*, pp. 113, 117, 118 and 139.

25. Barthes, *Image/Music/Text*, p. 143.

26. *Autobiography*, p. 13.

27. Mallarmé, *Oeuvres Complètes* (Paris, 1945), p. 366.

28. Lacan, 'Desire and the Interpretation of Desire in Hamlet', *Yale French Studies*, no. 55/56, p. 40.

29. *Prepositions*, pp. 65 and 158.

30. Lacan, 'Desire', p. 40.

31. Cox, 'Poetry of Louis Zukofsky', p. 142. For information about Reb Pinchos, see *Man and Poet*, pp. 35-6.

32. Barthes, *Image/Music/Text*, p. 142.

33. *All: the Collected Shorter Poems* (New York, 1971), p. 11. See H. Schimmel, 'Zuk. Yehoash David Rex', *Man and Poet*, p. 235-46.

34. Lacan, 'Desire', p. 23.

35. *Prepositions*, p. 39.

36. See *Man and Poet*, pp. 69-70.

37. S. Freud, *The Standard Edition of the Complete Psychological Works* (24 vols., London, 1951), vol. 14, p. 85.

38. Ibid., p. 198.

39. Interview with Zukofsky, *Contemporary Literature*, vol. 10, no. 2, p. 205.

40. Lacan, 'Desire', p. 39.

41. Freud, *Standard Edition*, vol. 14, p. 201.

42. *All*, p. 89.

43. Stokes, *Critical Writings*, vol. 2, p. 237.

44. C. Tomlinson in *Man and Poet*, p. 88.

45. Reported from a private telephone conversation in 1979.

46. *Carminalenia* (Manchester, 1980), p. 68.

47. *Bolshevism in Art* (Manchester, 1978), p. 215.

48. *Selected Poems of Mörike and Hölderlin* (New York, 1972), p. xxvii.

49. Cox, 'Poetry of Louis Zukofsky', p. 11.

50. My view of Mallarmé's hat is in co-operation with T. Hanson's article — 'Mallarmé's Hat', *Yale French Studies*, no. 54, pp. 214 ff.

BIBLIOGRAPHY

I Primary Texts

A. *Ezra Pound*

(i) Poetry

A Draft of XVI Cantos (Paris, 1925)
A Lume Spento (London, 1965)
Collected Early Poems (New York, 1976)
Collected Shorter Poems (London, 1973)
The Cantos of Ezra Pound (New York, 1970)
The Translations of Ezra Pound, ed. H. Kenner (London, 1963)

(ii) Prose

ABC of Reading (London, 1973)
Ezra Pound Speaking, ed. L. Doob (Westport, Conn., 1978)
Gaudier-Brzeska: a Memoir (London, 1960)
Guide to Kulchur (London, 1966)
Jefferson and/or Mussolini (London, 1935)
Letters of Ezra Pound, 1907-1941, ed. D.D. Paige (London, 1971)
Literary Essays, ed. T.S. Eliot (London, 1974)
Money Pamphlets by £ (London, 1951)
Pavannes and Divagations (London, 1958)
Pound/Joyce: the Letter of Ezra Pound to James Joyce, ed. F. Read, (London, 1967)
Selected Prose, ed. W. Cookson (London, 1973)

(iii) Other Texts

'America: Chances and Remedies', *New Age*, vol. 13, pp. 58 and 83.
'The Approach to Paris', *New Age*, Part I, 4 Sept. 1913; Part II, 11 Sept. 1913; Part III, 2 Oct. 1913
'How I Began', *T.P.'s Weekly*, 6 June, 1913, p. 707
Letters to William Bird, Bird Mss., Lilly Library, Indiana University
'Three Poems', *The European*, vol. 12, no. 5 (Jan. 1959)

B. James Joyce

Dubliners (London, 1967)
Finnegans Wake (London, 1971)
Letters of James Joyce, vol. I, ed. S. Gilbert (London, 1957)
Letters of James Joyce, vol. II, ed. R. Ellmann (London, 1966)
A Portrait of the Artist as a Young Man (London, 1971)
Ulysses (London, 1971)

C. H.D.

(i) Poetry

By Avon River (New York, 1949)
Helen in Egypt (New York, 1974)
Hermetic Definition (Oxford, 1972)
Red Roses for Bronze (London, 1931)
Trilogy (Cheadle, Cheshire, 1973)

(ii) Prose

End To Torment (New York, 1979)
Palimpsest (Carbondale, Illinois, 1968)
Tribute to Freud (Boston, 1974)

D. Louis Zukofsky

(i) Poetry

A (Berkeley, 1980)
A, 1-12 (London, 1966)
A, 12- 21 (London, 1969)
A, 22 & 23 (New York, 1971)
All: the Collected Shorter Poems (New York, 1971)
Catullus (with Celia Zukofsky) (New York, 1969)

(ii) Prose

Autobiography (New York, 1970)
Bottom: On Shakespeare (Austin, Texas, 1963)
An 'Objectivists' Anthology (editor) (Le Beausset, Var, 1932)
Prepositions (London, 1967)

II Critical and Biographical Material Relating to Primary Texts

A: Ezra Pound

Agenda, vol. 4, no. 2 (special issue on Pound's 80th birthday)

Brooke-Rose, C. *A ZBC of Ezra Pound* (London, 1971)

Carne-Ross, D.S. 'The Music of a Lost Dynasty: EP in the Classroom', *Boston University Journal* (Winter 1972)

Chace, W. *The Political Identities of Ezra Pound and T.S. Eliot* (Stanford, 1973)

Crozier, A. 'The Young Pound', *PN Review*, vol. 5, no. 2

Davie, D. *The Poet as Sculptor* (London, 1963)

Dekker, G. *Sailing After Knowledge* (London, 1963)

de Nagy, C. *The Poetry of Ezra Pound: the Pre-Imagist Stage* (Bern, 1968)

Durant, A.E. *Ezra Pound: Identity in Crisis* (Brighton, 1981)

Edwards J.H. and Vasse, W.V. *An Annotated Index to Cantos 1-84 (Berkeley, 1957)*

Ellmann, M. 'Floating the Pound', *Oxford Literary Review*, vol. 3, no. 3, pp. 16ff

Emery, C. *Ideas Into Action* (Miami, 1958)

Forrest-Thomson, V. 'Closed and Open Form: Some Reflections on Verse Techniques in Ezra Pound', unpublished

Gordon, D, 'The Azalea is Grown', *Paideuma*, vol. 4, pp. 223 ff

Hall, D. 'Interview with Ezra Pound', *Paris Review*, no. 28

Heymann, C.D. *Ezra Pound: the Last Rower* (London, 1976)

Jackson, T.H. *The Early Poetry of Ezra Pound* (Cambridge, Mass., 1968)

Kenner, H. *The Pound Era* (London, 1975)

Langumier, E. 'Scarabs and Gold', *Paideuma*, vol. 8, p. 57

MacNaughton, W, 'Pound: a Brief Memoir', *Paideuma*, vol. 3, pp. 322 ff

Mottram, E. 'Pound, Olson and the Golden Flower', *Chapman*, vol. 2, no. 2

M. Nänny, 'Oral Dimensions in Ezra Pound', *Paideuma*, vol. 6, pp. 13-26

—— *Ezra Pound: Poetics for an Electric Age* (Bern, 1973)

Nassar, E.P. *The Cantos of Ezra Pound: the Lyric Mode* (Johns Hopkins, 1975)

Norman, C. *Ezra Pound: a Biography* (London, 1969)

Pearlman, D.S. *The Barb of Time* (Oxford, 1969)

Pleynet, M. 'La Compromission Poétique', *Tel Quel*, no. 70, pp. 11 ff

Read, F. 'The Mathematical Symbolism of Ezra Pound's Revolutionary

Mind', *Paideuma*, vol. 7, pp. 7 ff, now in *'76: One World and the 'Cantos'* (North Carolina, 1981)

Reck, M. *Ezra Pound: a Close-up* (London, 1968)

—— 'A Conversation between Ezra Pound and Allen Ginsberg', *Evergreen Review* (June 1968)

Rosenthal, M. 'Pound at his Best: Canto 47 as a Model for Poetic Thought', *Paideuma*, vol. 6, pp. 309-21

Russell, P, (ed.) *An Examination of Ezra Pound* (New York, 1973)

Ruthven, K.K. *A Guide to Ezra Pound's Personae (1926)* (Berkeley, 1969)

Schneidau, H. 'Wisdom Past Metaphor', *Paideuma*, vol. 5, no. 1

Schuldiner, M. 'Pound's Progress in the Pisan Cantos', *Paideuma*, vol. 4, p. 77

Seelye, (ed.) *Charles Olson and Ezra Pound: an Encounter at St Elizabeths* (New York, 1975)

Simpson, D. 'Pound's Wordsworth', *ELH*, vol. 45, no. 4

Smith, P.H. and Durant, A.E. 'Pound's Metonymy: Canto 47 Revisited', *Paideuma*, vol. 8, pp. 327-33

Stock, N. (ed.) *Ezra Pound: Perspectives* (Chicago, 1965)

Stock, N. *The Life of Ezra Pound* (London, 1974)

Terrell, C.F. 'The Sacred Edict of K'ang Hsi', *Paideuma*, vol. 2, pp. 69 ff

Wilhelm, J.J. *The Later Cantos of Ezra Pound* (New York, 1977)

B: James Joyce

Beckett, S. *et al. Exagmination of his Factification for Incamination of work in progress* (London, 1972)

Bolderoff, F. *Hermes to his son Thoth* (Woodward, Penn., 1968)

Ellmann, R. *James Joyce* (Oxford, 1959)

—— *The Consciousness of Joyce* (London, 1977)

Heath, S. 'Ambiviolences', *Tel Quel*, no. 50 pp. 22-43; no. 51, pp. 64-77

—— 'Trames de la lecture', *Tel Quel*, no. 54, pp. 4-15

Levin, H. *James Joyce: a Critical Introduction* (London, 1960)

MacCabe, C. *James Joyce and the Revolution of the Word* (London, 1977)

Major, R. 'I am Joyce (Freud)', *Magazine Littéraire,* no. 161, pp. 41-2

C: H.D.

Contemporary Literature, vol. 10, no. 4 (special H.D. issue)

DuPlessis, R.B. 'Family, Sexes, Psyche: H.D.', *Montemora*, no. 6 (1979)

Friedman, S.S. 'Mythology, Psychoanalysis and the Occult in the Later

Poetry of H.D.' PhD thesis University of Wisconsin, 1973

Quinn, V. *Hilda Doolittle* (New York, 1967)

—— 'H.D.'s "Hermetic Definition;" the Poet as Archetypal Mother', *Contemporary Literature*, vol. 18, no. 1, pp. 51 ff

D: Louis Zukofsky

Ahearn B. 'Origins of A: Zukofsky's Materials for Collage', *ELH*, vol. 45, no. 1, pp. 152-76

Booth, M. *Catalogue of Zukofsky Manuscript Collection at HRC* (Austin, 1975)

Cox, K. 'The Poetry of Louis Zukofsky', *Montemora*, no 5 (1978)

Dembo, L.S. 'Interview with Louis Zukofsky', *Contemporary Literature*, vol. 10, no. 2, pp. 203 ff

Harmon, W. 'Eiron Eyes', *Parnassus: Poetry in Review* (Spring/Summer 1979), pp. 5-23

Maps, vol. 1, no. 5 (1973) (special Zukofsky issue)

Paideuma, vol. 7, no. 3 (special Zukofsky issue)

Terrell, C.F. (ed.) *Louis Zukofsky: Man and Poet* (Orono, 1980)

Zukofsky, C. *American Friends* (New York, 1979)

III Psychoanalytical Material

Bornemann, E. *The Psychoanalysis of Money* (New York, 1976)

Freud, S. *The Standard Edition of the Complete Psychological Works* (24 vols.) (London, 1951)

Lacan, J. *Ecrits* (Paris, 1966)

—— *The Four Fundamental Concepts of Psychoanalysis* (London, 1979)

—— *Le Séminaire XX: Encore* (Paris, 1975)

—— 'Desire and the Interpretation of Desire in Hamlet', *Yale French Studies*, no. 55/6 (1977)

Laplanche, J., and Leclaire, S. 'The Unconscious: a Psychoanalytical Study', *Yale French Studies*, no. 48 (1974)

—— and Pontalis, J-B. *The Language of Psychoanalysis* (London, 1973

Leclaire, S. *Psychanalyser* (Paris, 1968)

Lemaire, A. *Jacques Lacan* (London, 1977)

MacCabe, C. (ed.) *The Talking Cure* (London, 1981)

Mitchell, J. *Psychoanalysis and Feminism* (London, 1976)

Ruitenbeck, H.M. (ed.) *Psychoanalysis and Female Sexuality* (New

Haven, 1966)
Wilden, A. *The Language of the Self* (New York, 1968)

IV Other Critical, Biographical and Miscellaneous Works

Aldington, R. *Life for Life's Sake* (London, 1968)
Allenton, V. 'Ecriture Chinoise', *Tel Quel*, no. 48/9, pp. 47 ff
Barthes, R. *La Chambre Claire* (Paris, 1980)
—— *Le Degré Zéro de L'Ecriture* (Paris, 1972)
—— *Image/Music/Text* (London, 1977)
Bataille, G. *Oeuvres Complètes*, vol. 2 (Paris, 1970)
Beach, S. *Shakespeare & Co.* (London, 1960)
Beer, T. *The Mauve Decade* (Garden City, 1925)
Bryher *The Heart to Artemis* (London, 1962)
Coffman, S.K. Jr., *Imagism: a Chapter for the History of Modern Poetry* (New York, 1972)
Derrida, J. *Glas* (Paris, 1974)
—— *La Dissémination* (Paris, 1972)
—— *Writing and Difference* (London, 1978)
Eliot, T.S. *The Sacred Wood* (London, 1972)
Emerson, R.W. *Collected Works*, vol. 1 (Cambridge, Mass., 1971)
Empson, W. 'Rhythm and Imagery in English Poetry', *British Journal of Aesthetics* (January 1962)
Fender, S. *The American Long Poem* (London, 1977)
Fenollosa, E. *The Chinese Written Character as a Medium for Poetry* (City Lights, San Francisco, n.d.)
Forrest-Thomson, V. *Poetic Artifice: a Theory of Twentieth Century Poetry* (Manchester, 1978)
Gombrich, E.H. 'Icones Symbolicae', *Journal of the Warburg and Courtauld Institutes*, vol. 11 (1948)
Hanson, T. 'Mallarmé's Hat', *Yale French Studies*, no. 54 (1977)
Heath, S. 'Difference', *Screen*, vol. 19, no. 3, pp. 50-116
—— 'Language, Literature, Materialism', *Sub-Stance*, no. 17 (1977)
Herron, I.H. *The Small Town in American Literature* (New York, 1959)
Hofstadter, R. *The Age of Reform* (New York, 1961)
Homer *The Odyssey* (London, 1963)
Jackson, H. *The Eighteen-nineties* (London, 1922)
Jakobson, R. *Selected Writing*, vol. 2 (Hague, 1971)
Jensen, H. *Sign, Symbol and Script* (London, 1970)
Kristeva, J. *Desire in Language* (New York, 1980)

—— 'Signifying Practice and the Mode of Production', *Edinburgh Magazine,* no. 1 (1976)

—— 'The Semiotic Activity', *Screen*, vol. 14, no. 1/2, pp. 25-39

Lawrence, D.H. *Tales* (London, 1934)

Leavis, F.R. *New Bearings in English Poetry* (London, 1950)

Lidderdale, J., and Nicholson, M. *Dear Miss Weaver: Harriet Shaw Weaver, 1876-1961* (London, 1970)

Liebovici, M. 'La Position Féminine dans la Bible', *Tel Quel*, no. 74, pp. 24-9, and no. 75, pp. 100-4, and no. 76, pp. 94-100

Macciocchi, M.A. (ed.) *Eléments pour une analyse du fascisme* (2 vols. Paris, 1976)

Mallarmé, S. *Oeuvres Complètes* (Paris, 1945)

Marx, K. *The Class Struggles in France 1848-1850* (New York, 1972)

—— *The Eighteenth Brumaire of Louis Bonaparte* (New York, 1963)

—— and Engels, F. *Selected Works* (Moscow, 1962)

Mehlman, J. *Revolution and Repetition* (Berkeley, 1977)

Middleton, C. *Bolshevism in Art* (Manchester, 1978)

—— *Carminalenia* (Manchester, 1980)

—— *Selected Poems of Mörike and Hölderlin* (Chicago, 1972)

Mulvey, L. and Wollen, P. 'The Riddles of the Sphinx: a script', *Screen,* vol. 18, no. 2, pp. 61-77

Murray, M.A. *Ancient Egyptian Legends* (London, 1913)

Reich, W. *The Mass Psychology of Fascism* (New York, 1970)

Riddel, J.N. *The Inverted Bell: Modernism and the Counterpoetics of W.C. Williams* (Baton Rouge, 1974)

—— 'Decentering the Image' in J.V. Harari (ed.), *Textual Strategies* (London, 1979)

Sinclair, M. 'Two Notes', *The Egoist* 1 June 1915

Smith, H.N. *The Virgin Land* (New York, 1950)

Stokes, A. *The Critical Writings* (3 vols., London, 1978)

Swinburne, A.C. *Poems and Ballads* (1st Series) (London, 1896)

Symons, A. *Dramatis Personae* (Indianapolis, 1896)

—— *Silhouettes* (London, 1892)

Williams, W.C. *Autobiography* (New York, 1967)

—— *Imaginations* (New York, 1971)

Ziff, L. *The American Eighteen-nineties* (London, 1967)

INDEX

Adams, John 30, 65
Agostino, 46
Aldington, Richard 107
Althusser, Louis 41
Amen 119, 125
American Seal, the 87-9
anality, 79-82, 89, 90, 92-5, 97, 102, 105

Baller, F.W. 66
Balzac, Honoré de 113
Barnes, Djuna 109
Barthes, Roland 27, 142-3, 161
Bataille, Georges 87-9, 94-5
Beach, Sylvia 107
Beer, Thomas 83
Bion, 49
Bird, William 55, 90
Bolderoff, Frances 105
Brooke-Rose, Christine 24, 47
Browning, Robert 7-9
Bryher 108, 122

Carne-Ross, D.S. 54
castration 52-4, 76, 78, 81, 84, 90-3, 102-3, 109, 116
Cavalcanti 44-6, 60
Chace, William 72
Chambers, Whittaker 164
Chaucer, Geoffrey 140
Coleridge, S.T.C. 102
Confucius 72
Cox, Kenneth 135, 143
Crozier, Andrew 17-18
cummings, e.e. 138

Davie, Donald 30, 43, 47, 54, 58
Decadents, The 7-8, 10-11
Derrida, Jacques 3, 62, 87-9, 159
Doob, L.W. 58
Doolittle, Charles 112, 114-16
Doolittle, Hilda (H.D.) 1, 3, 20, 47, 77, 110-32, 148
    By Avon River 118-19
    End to Torment 47, 111-13, 115, 117, 123, 125, 129, 131

Helen in Egypt 118-25, 129
Hermetic Definition 111, 119, 129-31
    'Notes on Thought and Vision' 119
    'Oread' 20
    Palimpsest 122
    Red Roses for Bronze 119
    Tribute to Freud 112, 114-16, 119, 121; 'Advent' 112, 115, 119
    Trilogy 119, 120, 126-8
Douglas, Major 72
drunkenness 94, 97
Duncan, Ronald 63
Durand, Lionel 130-1
Durant, A.E. 2, 81-2, 158

editing 33, 90, 97, 105, 110-11, 118
Ellmann, Maud 2, 80
Ellmann, Richard 97, 100
Emerson, Ralph Waldo 70-1, 82-4, 89
Emery, Clark 58
Empson, William 21
eye/eyesight 11-12, 83-4, 87, 89, 90-2, 94, 97-8, 112-13, 135, 147
    evil eye 95
    pineal eye 89, 94, 153

fasces 23, 64, 69, 87
Fenollosa, Ernest 60-4, 82
Fleming, William 61
Fletcher, John Gould 21
fort/da game 116-17, 123
Franklin, Benjamin 71
Freud, Sigmund 47, 51-2, 61, 71-2, 80-1, 83, 93, 108-16 *passim*, 120-3, 126, 130, 143-6

Gaudier-Brzeska, Henri 46, 63
Gilgamesh, The Epic of 140, 164
Gould, George 92

Hall, Donald 79, 81
Hanson, Thomas 153
Heath, Stephen 97, 104, 129, 163